FUN WITH ELECTRIC TRAINS

BY JIM KELLY
ASSOCIATE EDITOR

Model Railroader

D1856193

EDITOR: Michael Emmerich
ART DIRECTOR: Lawrence Luser
ARTIST: Mark Watson
ASSISTANT EDITOR: Marcia Stern

Distributed by:
Airlife Publishing Ltd.
101 Longden Road, Shrewsbury SY3 9EB, England

Published by Kalmbach Publishing Co., 21027 Crossroads Circle, P. O. Box 1612, Waukesha, WI 53187. Printed in the U. S. A. Library of Congress Catalog Card Number: 89-64150. ISBN: 0-89024-098-1.

Train Sizes

Electric trains come in different shapes and sizes. Some locomotives you can hide in the palm of your hand; others you'd have trouble stuffing into a shoebox.

In this book we'll look at the four train sizes most beginners are likely to have: HO, N, G, (also called "large scale" or "LGB"), and Lionel O27 (often simply called "Lionel").

For now let's just divide these four sizes into three broad categories. LGB and Lionel are large trains; HO trains are small; N trains are tiny. The picture shows them actual size — and that pretty much says it all.

Scale and Gauge

Two words are used in discussing train sizes — "scale" and "gauge." Scale is the ratio of the model's size to the real thing. HO scale trains, for example, are 1/87th the size of real trains.

Gauge means how far apart the rails are, measured inside to inside. HO gauge rails are 16.5 mm apart (about $5/8$").

We'll go into detail in the chapters on the individual sizes. For now, just keep in mind that the scale designations cover families of products that can be used together regardless of who made them. An engine made by A should be able to pull cars made by B, on track made by C, and so on and so on.

N

HO

Lionel O27

G (also called "large scale" or "LGB")

Deep carpet can be mighty tough going for small electric trains.

Keep 'Em Running

Electric train sets have been around since about 1900, so it could be your grandfather — perhaps even his father — received a train set for Christmas. Probably he set it up to run round and round under the Christmas tree. That was fine and dandy for him but might not work out well for you. His trains were large (the small ones had not been invented yet) and he probably did not have a plush rug (those had not been invented either).

Stay Off the Rug

Don't try to run HO or N scale trains on the carpet. First of all, you will have lots of problems keeping the trains on the track because the track would not be firmly supported. Additionally, there's an excellent chance that carpet fuzz and maybe even cat hair will get into your locomotive's mechanism and bollix it up altogether.

The large trains (LGB and Lionel) are fine on regular carpet, but beware of shags and fuzzy types. For best results with any train size run your trains on a smooth, hard surface. For now a hardwood, tile, or linoleum floor is fine. So's the kitchen counter or a table. Eventually you may want to build a train board. A later chapter offers some ideas on those.

Cleaning Rails and Wheels

Hobby dealers tell me the number one problem they see is dirty wheels and dirty track. Dirt and gunk block out the electricity, preventing its flow from the rail to the wheel. Think about how small a wheel's "footprint" on the rail is, and you can understand why dirt is such a worthy opponent.

For cleaning any size track I recommend a track cleaning block available at hobby shops. Bright Boy is one popular brand, but there are many others.

Liquid cleaners are also available, but I'm less keen on these. If you use one you should apply only a few drops and wipe your track off carefully and completely with a rag. Otherwise the cleaner can be transferred to the car wheels where it can capture dirt and produce gunk buildups that cause derailments.

Plastic wheels are especially vulnerable to dirt and gunk. Eventually you might have to clean all the wheels, and if you have more than a handful of cars, that's no fun at all. To clean wheels take them all out and scrub them with soap and water, using a toothbrush. Rinse and dry them before reinstalling.

Like we were saying, it's best to avoid dirty wheel problems in the first place by never using any oily substance on your track.

Cleaning Engine Wheels

The cleaner you keep your track the less trouble you'll have with locomotive wheels getting dirty. Unless there's a lot of dust in your air, you should have to clean the locomotive wheels rarely, maybe only once or twice a year — maybe never.

One way to clean locomotive wheels is with Q-tips, or another brand of cotton swabs, and rubbing alcohol or a household cleaner like Fantastic or Formula 409. Clean those parts of the wheels you can reach, then set the engine on the track momentarily to turn the wheels and expose portions you couldn't reach before.

Whether to Oil

Hobby dealers tell us beginners many times want to know if they should oil their engine. As long as your engine runs well, don't. "If it ain't broke, don't fix it," is a good electric trains philosophy. Real engineers in the days of steam were always working the thumb on the old squirt can, but we should never oil just for the sake of oiling.

At the same time be aware that some engines are not lubricated at the factory because the manufacturer fears the oil will drift from the mechanism onto the outside of the model or the packaging and spoil it. Obviously such a model should be oiled, but *sparingly*.

The biggest problem you'll face with lubricating an engine properly is that usually you have to take off the body to do it. Most of the time this is easy, but sometimes it's amazingly difficult. Make sure you keep any drawings or directions that came with the engine, since the secret is often revealed there.

Diesel body shells are held on by tabs somewhere near the middle. Lay the engine on its back on a folded towel, foam pad, or something else to protect it. You'd still like to have a horn on top when this is over! Spread the sides with your thumbnails, or if you prefer, pry them away with small screwdrivers or toothpicks. Pull the mechanism out carefully.

What to Oil

To sum it up, you should oil the motor bearings, drive shaft bearings, and the gears — and you should do it very, very lightly. Bearings are those little metal doughnuts within which motor and drive shafts turn. Gears are — well, you already know what gears are.

The motor bearings are particularly important, and you need to be especially careful here. Any oil that seeps inside the motor can damage it. A toothpick makes a good applicator and will not permit you to over-oil.

To oil the gears place just one small drop on one gear in a gear system. When you put your engine back on the track, run it slowly for half a minute or so to let the oil spread to the gear surfaces evenly without being thrown around inside the engine or onto your track.

What Oil to Use

When you lubricate use a special train oil available at your hobby shop. Make sure you buy one that won't harm plastics. LaBelle's No. 108 is a good choice, but there are many others. Household oils (like 3-in-1) are usually too heavy, especially for HO and N trains, and they can harm plastics.

Don't oil the axles on cars, as that will just lead to dirt buildup. If a wheel is so squeaky it sounds as if you're transporting mice, try swapping the wheel sets around in the car. If the squeaking persists, oil just the offending axle.

Remember, when it comes to oiling trains, don't unless it becomes absolutely necessary, then sneak up on the job real careful. Just a little oil goes a long, long way.

Abrasive block cleaners like the Walthers Bright Boy are simple but effective tools for cleaning track.

Cotton swabs are a good tool for cleaning locomotive wheels.

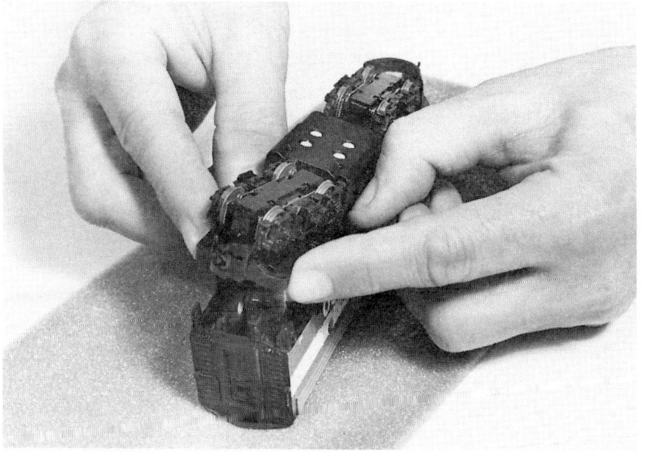
Just about all diesel locomotive bodies can be removed by spreading the sides slightly so notches in the body will clear the tabs on the mechanism.

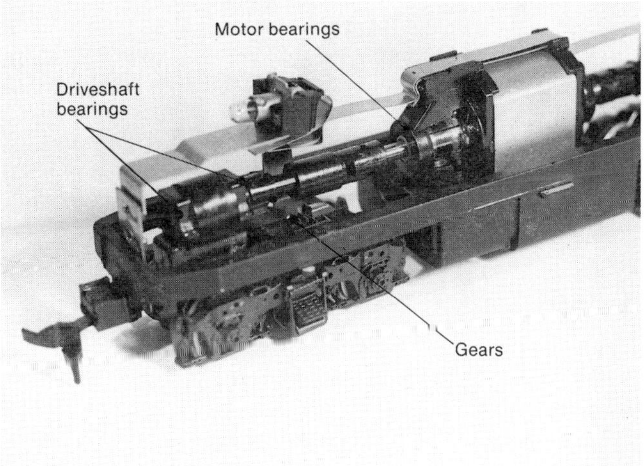

The lubrication points are those places where moving surfaces touch one another.

This paper backdrop desert scene adds distance, and is available at most hobby shops.

Getting Started in HO

About 80 percent of you are getting started in HO scale, so you are in the majority. Because there's strength in numbers you have a broader range of products available than those working in any other train size. Sometimes it almost seems as if you have too many choices!

Just to give you some idea, every year Walthers, the largest model train supply distributor, publishes an 800-page HO catalog nearly an inch thick. Your hobby dealer likely has one you can look at, and though it's the most inclusive reference available, it still doesn't show everything! Probably there's another fifty-pages worth that Walthers doesn't carry.

The Boom Scale

HO is pronounced as two separate letters, "aitch-oh," not ho, as in Santa Claus laughing.

When the size was introduced back in the thirties HO meant half-O, O being the most popular size at that time. For a lot of complicated reasons HO trains really aren't half the size of O anymore, but they are close. Basically HO trains are 1/87th the size of real trains.

HO scale took off like a rocket after World War Two, mostly because these were trains small enough to set up somewhere in average-sized homes and affordable enough for average-sized pocketbooks.

Every year approximately one million HO train sets are sold during the Christmas season. The good news is that lots and lots of people, particularly young people, are introduced to the train hobby with these inexpensive sets. The bad news is that many of these sets are poorly made and don't hold up well.

The hobby shops tell us that every year they see lots of HO train set buyers who have decided they like HO trains but wonder if better quality is available. The answer is a resounding yes — and you don't have to pay a lot to get it. Good quality in HO costs only a little more than bad — sometimes it even costs less! It's just a matter of knowing what's good and what isn't, an area in which your dealer should be able to help you.

Better Locomotives

Many hobby dealers recommended Athearn's diesel locomotives as the best choice for HO modelers wanting to upgrade. These are well made with sturdy metal frames and large motors. They pick up current and are powered on all wheels. Most are priced under $30. Replacement parts are fairly easy to find.

A great engine for beginners is the Athearn F7. It'll run fine on the 18″-radius curves beginners usually use, provided you leave off the brake cylinders that are included as extra, glue-on parts.

Two other Athearn locomotives dealers recommended are the GP9 and the GP35. These are inexpensive and also work well on 18″-radius curves. One problem with these and

Big scenes on small HO layouts are no problem. This shot was taken on the Gold Hill Central, built by the staff of MODEL RAILROADER to celebrate its fiftieth anniversary.

The Kitty Hawk Central is a beginner's layout with an optional addition. (See the book *All Aboard: The Practical Guide to HO Model Railroading* for more information.)

Athearn's excellent HO F7 is a good engine to replace the one that came in your train set. We left the detail parts off the trucks because they cause problems on 18″-radius curves.

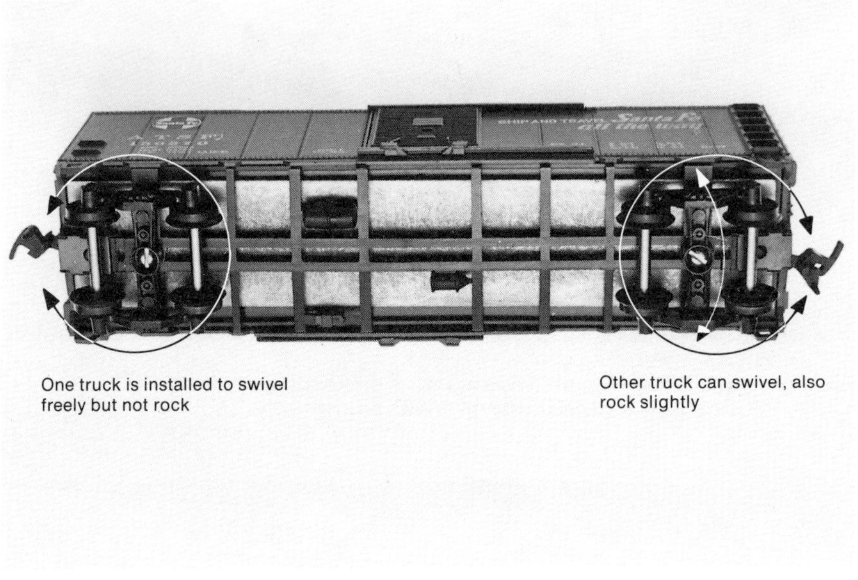

Good freight car performance.

Here's what you get in an Athearn boxcar kit. Assembly takes just a few minutes, and requires only a small screwdriver.

many other Athearn engines is that the handrails are included in the box but must be added by the modeler. Doing so isn't too tough, though — your dealer may have helpful hints. Besides, no one has ever been jailed for just leaving them off, and lots of modelers do.

As long as you're using 18″-radius curves, you're much better off to stay with smaller locomotives. It's harder to keep the big guys (particularly those with six wheels in each truck) on the track. Also the ends of long locomotives swing out so far on curves that they tend to come uncoupled or pull the car behind off the track.

If you'd like to buy a quality diesel locomotive that's ready to put on the track and go (handrails and all), then Atlas has an excellent product. These are made in Japan by Kato. They run even quieter and smoother than Athearn, but cost twice as much.

Incidentally, we recommend that beginners stick with diesels until they've gained experience, just because steam locomotives are more complex creatures. They have lots more moving parts and are more finicky. Certainly they won't stand up so well to the abuse a youngster can dish out.

If, however, you're a steam lover and want to start right out with it, both Mantua and Bowser make good, ready-to-run engines. Again, choose smaller locomotives that won't have trouble with the 18″-radius curves.

Better Cars

Poor-quality cars is another problem frequently seen in HO train sets. Sometimes the problem is simple — the cars just don't weigh enough to stay on the track. Adding a fishing weight or two can work wonders.

Sometimes, though, the problem is simply poor quality: The wheels aren't round, the trucks don't swivel freely, and so forth. Your hobby dealer may have replacement parts to solve some of these problems, but it's best to avoid these brands in the future.

When it comes to buying new cars, dealers again recommended the Athearn brand highly. These come as kits, but are easy to assemble. The only tool required is a screwdriver. Start with a boxcar, since about all you have to do is slip the floor into the body and mount the trucks with screws.

The one problem with HO we don't have an easy answer for is the couplers. It's difficult to think of anything good to say about the couplers that come with the equipment. They exert enough sideways pressure to contribute to derailments and are difficult to uncouple.

If you decide to get more deeply into HO, and particularly if you want to get into switching, you will want to consider converting to Kadee couplers. These fit easily into the coupler boxes on Athearn and other popular cars. Your hobby shop should have some you can look at.

Track

We recommend you use sectional track for your first layout and that you keep it flat and simple.

Atlas is the leader among HO track manufacturers and its products are generally good as well as easy to find. The turnouts don't always work perfectly, so if you have a problem, refer to our chapter on track.

Atlas has an excellent little book, *Blueprints for Atlas Snap-Track Layouts,* which you should definitely buy. It gives you a rundown on the track pieces available and insights on how to use them.

Atlas curved sections come in 3 standard radii, 15", 18", and 22". In each instance it takes six sections to complete a semicircle. Lots of dealers asked me to warn you away from the 15" curves. Forget you ever even knew they existed — they're too tight for most locomotives and cars. It's tempting to use some just so you can slip in one more track you'd like to have, but don't do it.

Brass and Nickel Silver

Atlas makes identical track pieces in brass and nickel silver. In case you're not sure what you have, if the metal is yellow, that's brass. For the reasons that follow we recommend nickel silver.

- Because of its color, nickel silver looks more realistic.
- Your train should run somewhat better with nickel silver. Both metals are excellent electrical conductors, but the oxide that forms on brass does not conduct as well as the one that forms on nickel silver. Consequently you have to clean the brass more often to maintain good electrical contact.

If you got started with brass, there's no problem in adding on with nickel silver. Probably no one will even notice. Nickel silver costs a few cents more per section, but given its advantages is certainly worth it.

This Alco RS-11 is representative of the fine-quality Atlas locomotives made by Kato.

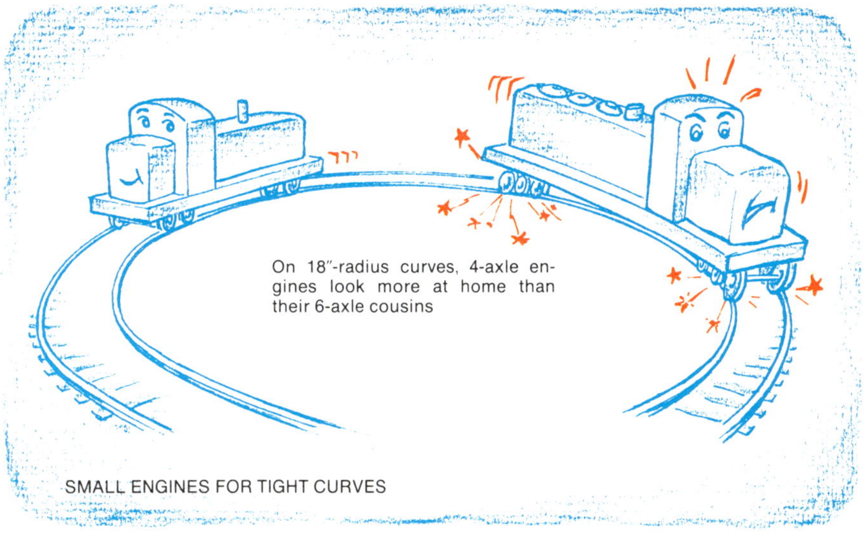

Many train sets today include galvanized steel track. If you're wondering, test with a magnet. Steel is magnetic; brass and nickel silver are not. Again, there's no problem with using this track with the others. We recommend you do not buy more of it, though, because someday you might want to solder wires to your rails, and that's more difficult with galvanized steel.

About Switches

You can buy your switches with electric switch machines included, but for the small layouts we're discussing in this book, they really aren't needed and just add more wiring and work. To make them look good you need to drill a hole in the train board and run the wires underneath. If later on you should decide you want machines after all, you can always buy and attach them, since Atlas sells them separately. Atlas also has a machine you can mount under the table.

Your hobby shop dealer will have switches other than Atlas and as long as they're HO you can use them. Look out for one problem, though. Some of these feature what is called a "live frog" design that requires additional layout wiring. Shinohara and Peco are two brands you might see that fall into this category.

If you want to run your trains with just one set of feeder wires, you need to stick with turnouts that have plastic or insulated frogs.

Track

Because it's so easy to use we recommend sectional track to beginners and used it on all the layouts we built for this book. You can't go wrong as long as you take time to understand the geometry of the track you're using and don't try to force it into shapes it just can't assume.

If six track sections are required to make a half-circle, then six it will have to be. Five or seven might look okay, but it won't be. There'll be kinks at each joint and those will cause derailments.

If the straight sections on one side of a loop add up to 36″, the straights on the other side will need to do the same. Your eye might be fooled, but the train won't be — and it'll derail. In short, go with the flow; don't force the track.

Also, avoid getting too fancy. Some beginner train sets feature over-and-under figure-8 track layouts. These can be fun to watch and the picture on the box looks neat, but generally such layouts don't work well because the track is not firmly supported and the grades are just too steep for reliable running. For your first layout we recommend no grades at all — keep it flat and keep it simple until you've gained experience.

Work Carefully

Laying sectional track is so easy we can get in a hurry and make some fundamental mistakes. Make sure as you go along that the rail ends are slipping entirely inside the rail joiners, not just catching on one side. Also make sure you have a joiner on every joint — it's surprisingly easy to leave one out. (We know — we forgot joiners several times on the HO layout!)

Check for good alignment as you lay track by running your thumb along the top of the rail. If your thumb feels a bump, the train will feel it too — and jump the track.

Usually the track comes with one rail joiner already attached at each end, and you don't need any tools to

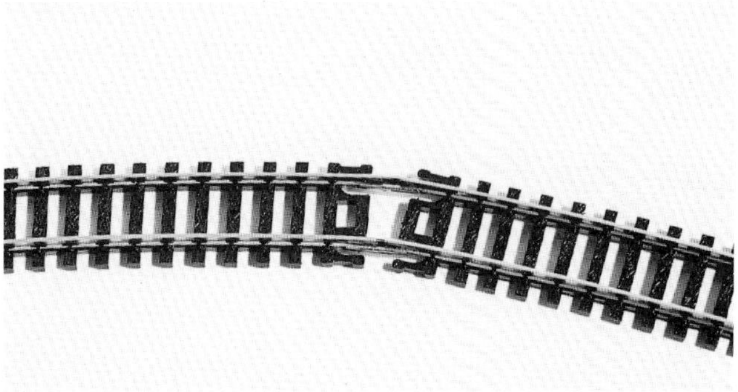

This is a kink, and a bad one at that. Kinks cause derailments, especially on curves, and can be hard to see. It helps to get your head down and sight along the track at train level.

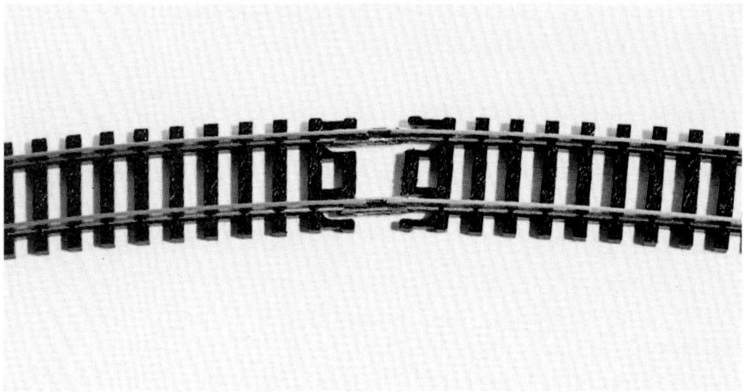

Gaps between rail ends are the other most frequent derailment-causers. Keep checking your track work as you go along so no gaps creep in.

We didn't have to fake this photo. Despite our best efforts in building our HO railroad we managed to get one rail end on top of a joiner instead of inside it.

The old thumb test. If your thumb feels a bump, the train will feel it too.

shove the pieces together. Eventually, particularly if you take your track apart and put it back together often, you may need to replace some joiners with new ones bought at your hobby shop. Make sure they're metal. Your dealer also has plastic ones, but those are for isolating tracks electrically, something we don't get into in this book.

With HO and N you need to fasten the track down with track nails available from your hobby shop. Otherwise the track will slip and slide around and the rail joints will work loose and start tripping up the trains.

If you work carefully you can drive the nails with an ordinary hammer, although a nailset is handy for that last easy tap or two.

Don't drive the nails down too firmly against the tops of the ties or they can distort the track. If your plan is temporary, just use a few nails here and there.

Switches

Eventually you'll probably want to do more than run in circles and will want to add a switch or two. A little lingo will help you figure out the kinds of switches you want.

Most switches (we also call them turnouts) have a straight leg that allows the train to go straight through and a curved leg to send the train off on a diverging route. The route the train takes is determined by a pair of short, movable rails, called points.

Imagine yourself standing in front of the switch and looking into it. If the curved leg goes off to your right, it's a right-hand switch. If the curve is to the left, it's a lefty. If both legs curve about equally, it's a wye.

You may see more complicated turnouts at your hobby shop — three-way and slip switches for example — but we strongly recommend against these. Even advanced model railroaders find them difficult to use and try to avoid them.

Turnout Woes

Usually when a switch causes trouble, it's the switch's fault, not yours. They are complex little creatures and somctimes aren't made as well as they should be. This holds true particularly in the small sizes.

The first thing to do if an engine or car is derailing at a switch is to run the equipment through slowly over and over again until you see exactly where the wheel is going off and can figure out why. Make sure you have

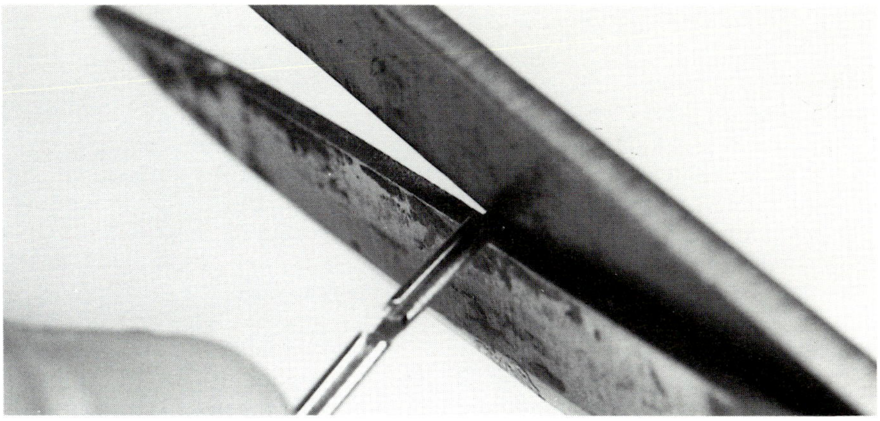

An old pair of scissors (or a new pair if no one is looking) works effectively for cutting rail joiners apart.

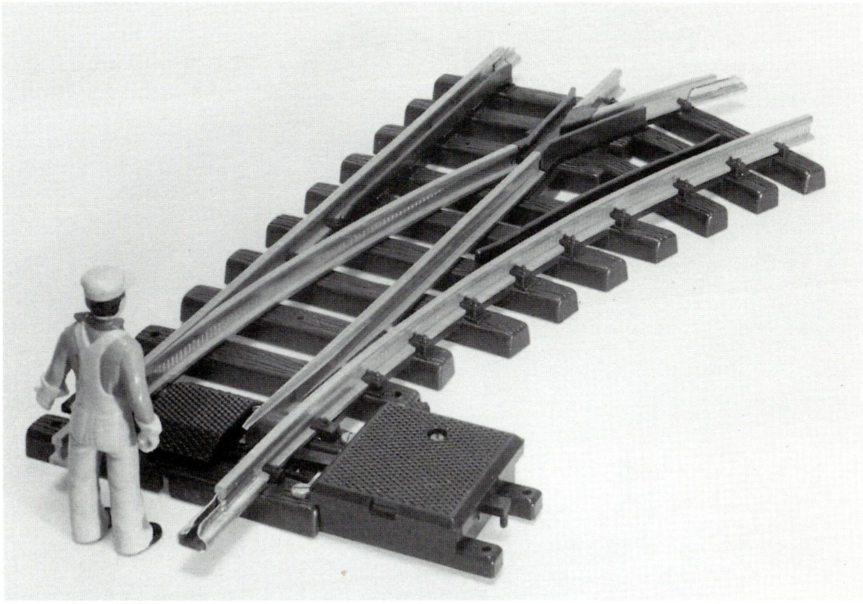

The curved leg goes off to the right, so this is a right-hand switch.

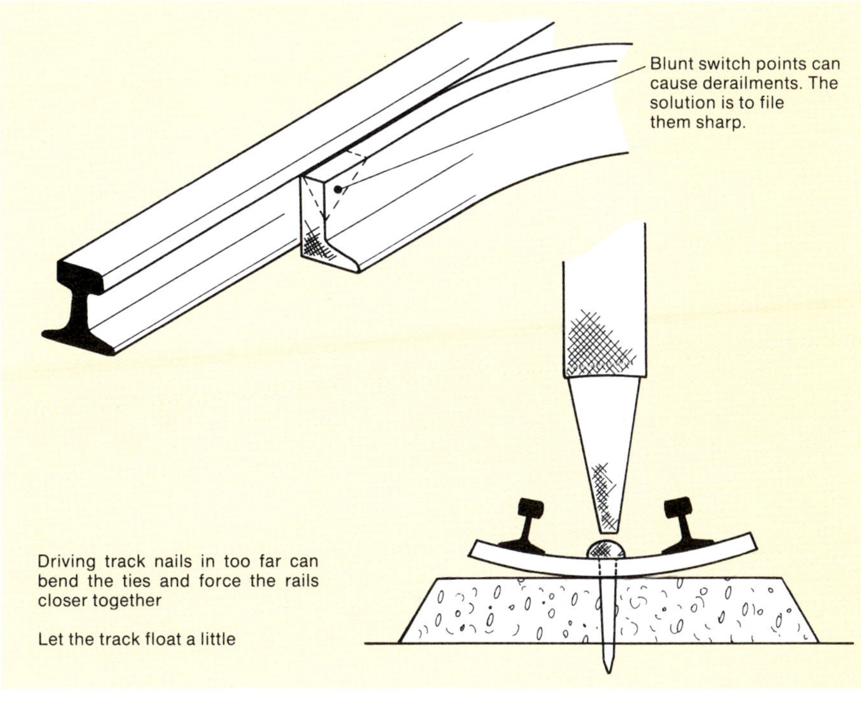

plenty of light so you can see exactly what's happening.

The most common cause of derailments is blunt points. The wheel hits them and bumps up and over the point, rather than being guided by it. The cure for this is to carefully file the point until it is in fact pointed and can do its job properly.

Because turnouts are made of a combination of metal rail and plastic castings, you'll occasionally find turnouts where these components don't line up evenly across the top. Carefully file down the high parts with a large (8″ or 10″ is good), flat file.

Buy the Good Stuff

The best solution to all these problems is to purchase better turnouts to begin with. All LGB and Lionel 027 switches are good quality, but the story is different with HO and N.

We've used Atlas track and turnouts on the HO and N layouts built for this book because we know that's what most beginners use. The products are good, although you can run into some of the problems we have noted above. They are reasonably priced, and just about every hobby shop carries them.

Atlas also has excellent, inexpensive books explaining how to use its track and your dealer probably has those. We recommend them highly.

Beware of track and switches at bargain prices. Track is like anything else — you usually get what you pay for. Frankly, good track can have problems enough; bad track is no bargain at any price.

When you buy turnouts make sure your dealer understands you want to be able to use them without having to do any special wiring. In most instances you can, although there are a few (usually more expensive types) you can't.

Switch Machines

Often you can buy your switches with built-in electric switch machines, but we recommend against them. You'll have to wire them, of course, and they have a way of burning out. Besides, on a small layout it's no problem to throw the turnouts by hand. If you're using Atlas switches, you can always buy the machines separately and add them later if you decide you want them.

Once again, we want you to have fun with electric trains, so we hope you'll keep your first layout simple. Walk before you fly.

A little filing can eliminate high spots in a turnout and produce an end to derailments.

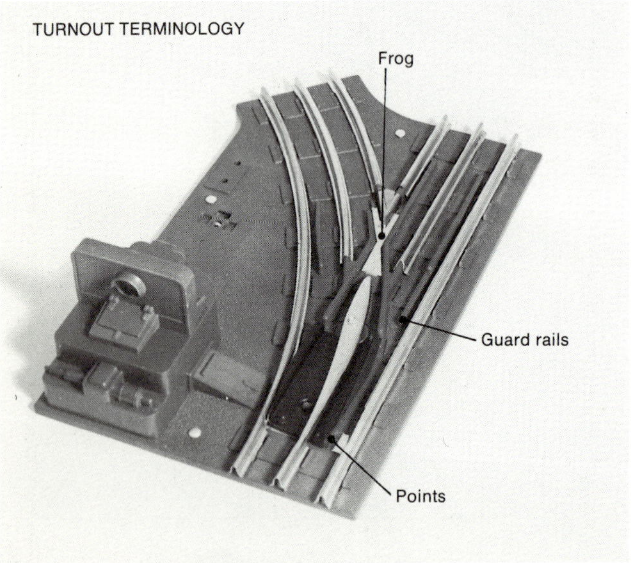

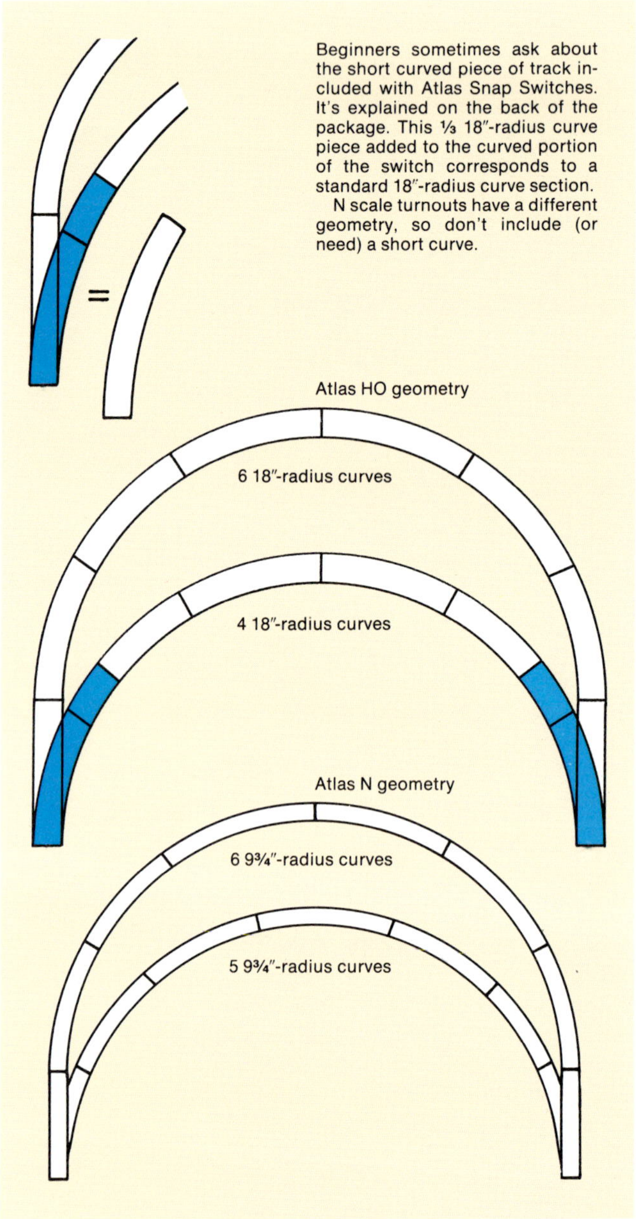

Locomotives

The simple truth is that many HO and N scale train set locomotives aren't very good. Hobby dealers say they see lots of frustrated beginners who want to know if something better is available. The answer is "absolutely." We'll make specific recommendations in later chapters; here we'll talk in general about what makes a good locomotive.

Quality in any scale means good looks and good performance, and it's usually in the performance category that purchasers are disappointed. If the train doesn't look good it won't sell, but performance is something you can't see until you take the engine out of the box.

We want our locomotives to run smoothly and stay on the track. Locomotives with the following characteristics are more likely to do so:

- Heavier is better, so look for hefty metal frames. Heavy locomotives will pull more cars, stay on the track better, and run smoother.

Electrical contact is better just because the weight presses the wheels more firmly against the rails. That's why keeping N scale track clean is so critical, whereas LGB and Lionel will plow through just about anything.

- The more powered wheels the better. This simply makes the engine more powerful and smoother running.
- The more wheels picking up electricity the better. This just means the motor gets a smoother flow of electricity and runs better. Also, as you add switches to a layout you'll find that not all the wheels can be touching metal all the time when an engine runs through. Some of the time the wheels will be touching plastic, so the more "live" wheels you have, the better.

This, incidentally, is a good reason for beginners to stay away from small switch or industrial engines, particularly in the small scales. They like to stall at turnouts.

Metal being better, it's best to avoid engines with rubber traction tires on some of the wheels, although many good locomotives have them. On poor-quality models these tires compensate for weight that should have been built into the locomotive in the first place. Also, the rubber is an insulator, so these wheels can't pick up electricity, except now and then on the flange.

- Expect a good engine to run quietly. You like your locomotive to run quiet for the same reason you like your car to run quiet. It's a sign that all is well and the locomotive is well made with a good motor and good gears that mesh properly and aren't devouring themselves.

Please keep in mind that some very good locomotives may not meet all the criteria here, and some products that do may fall short because of poor workmanship. If it walks like a turkey and gobbles like a turkey, it's a turkey.

Our 4 x 6-foot HO railroad features a farm on one corner, the Cornfield County International Airport on the other.

The Cornbelt Central

The two planes (Piper Cubs) come with the Revell Hangar kit. We painted them with spray can enamels to add a dash of color to this corner of the layout. The sailplane, by Noch, comes ready to glide.

You could easily build our 4 x 6-foot HO layout in less than a week, working an hour or two each evening. We hope you'll agree it beats the heck out of a loop of track on the floor.

The Train Board

We built the train board for our HO layout from three 2 x 4-foot ½″ plywood panels, even though we knew it would be easier to use one 4 x 6-foot piece.

In this age of smaller and smaller automobiles, though, few of us have the means to transport 4-foot-wide plywood sheets. We wanted to see for ourselves just what sorts of problems might be encountered with the smaller panels, and we're glad we did. Here's what to look out for.

First of all, don't trust the panels to be sized correctly or have square corners. Some of ours were off as much as ¼" in one or more dimensions. If you build a frame measuring exactly 4 x 6 feet and expect the top to fit nicely, you might be in for an unpleasant surprise. (I'm afraid that happened to us.)

The better method is to lay the three panels out on the floor, discovering the combination that will give the straightest sides and squarest corners.

Measure and cut the side framing pieces to length. Then measure the ends, remembering to subtract the width of the side members.

We assembled our train board with 1½"-long drywall screws, running them in with a crosshead screwdriver attachment for an electric drill. You don't need to drill a pilot hole for these screws, except near the ends of boards where they might split out.

Screw construction is fast and sure. We prefer it, but it's certainly not essential. You could also glue and nail the train board together, using white glue and finishing nails. Sometimes you have to be a little patient with glue/nail construction, particularly if your boards are a bit warped. You may have to let one joint set up before nailing the next so you don't have one corner coming loose while you're nailing another. Keep in mind that the glue is what holds the train board together; the nails are just a means of holding the joints closed until the glue sets.

When the train board frame is finished, *turn it over* before adding the top. This is important because it gives you the flattest surface with the flushest joints to work on.

Once our train board was finished we gave it two heavy coats of flat tan latex paint. This gives a nice, finished appearance even if you decide not to add scenery.

Track

If you have no track to start out with, the Atlas starter set is an excellent value. To make the Cornbelt Central you need only purchase the few extra pieces shown in the track list.

With time you could add several more switches and sidings to the CC. We particularly like the idea of

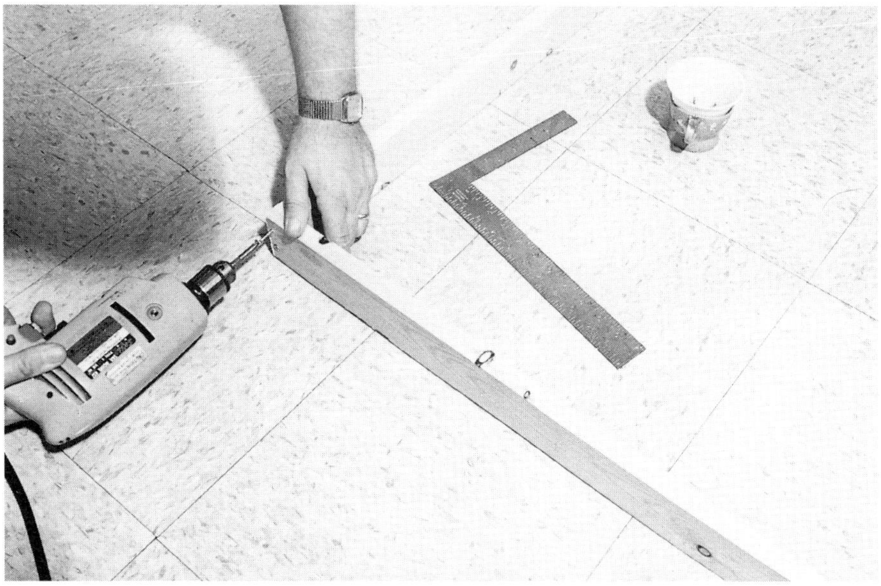

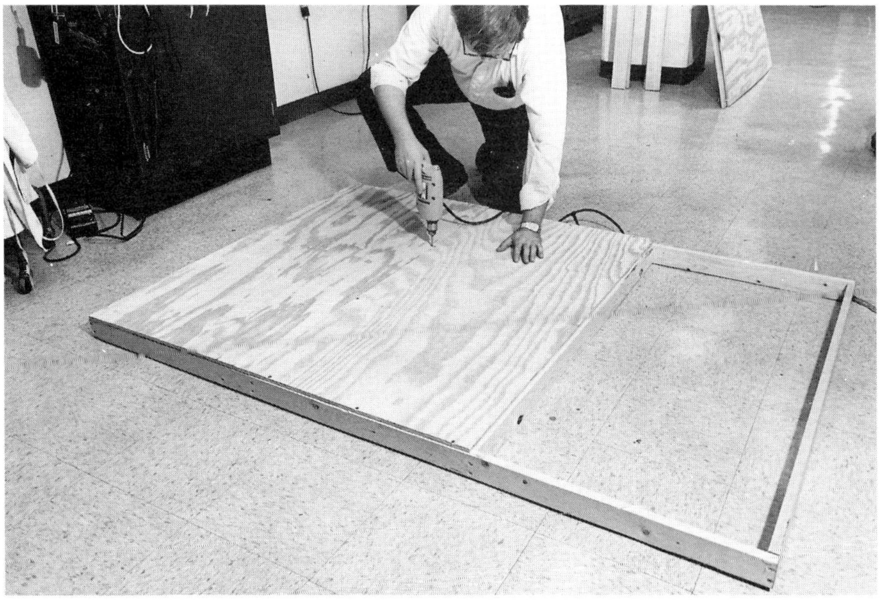

Our train board consists of three 2 x 4-foot panels mounted on a frame made of 1 x 3s. We drilled pilot holes in the ends of the sides so the wood wouldn't split out.

The materials you'll need to build the Cornbelt Central are listed below.

CORNBELT CENTRAL
Track (all Atlas)
12 No. 152 18″-radius curves
9 No. 150 9″ straights
2 No. 843 rail bumpers
2 No. 860 switches
3 No. 835 ⅓ 18″-radius curves
1 No. 847 track assortment (for 2 2½″ straights)
1 No. 842 terminal rail joiners
1 No. 844 rerailer
or
1 No. 88 starter set
3 No. 150 9″ straights
1 No. 835 ⅓ 18″-radius curve
1 No. 847 track assortment (for 2 2½″ straights)
1 No. 842 terminal rail joiners
1 No. 844 rerailer
Structures
1 IHC No. 812 barn
1 Model Power No. 433 farm house
1 IHC No. 4101 rural station
1 Revell No. 2001 hangar with 2

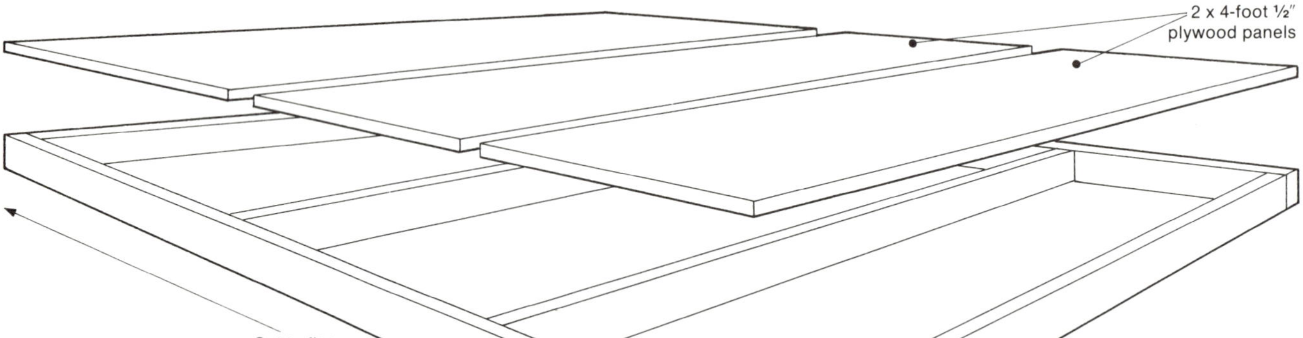

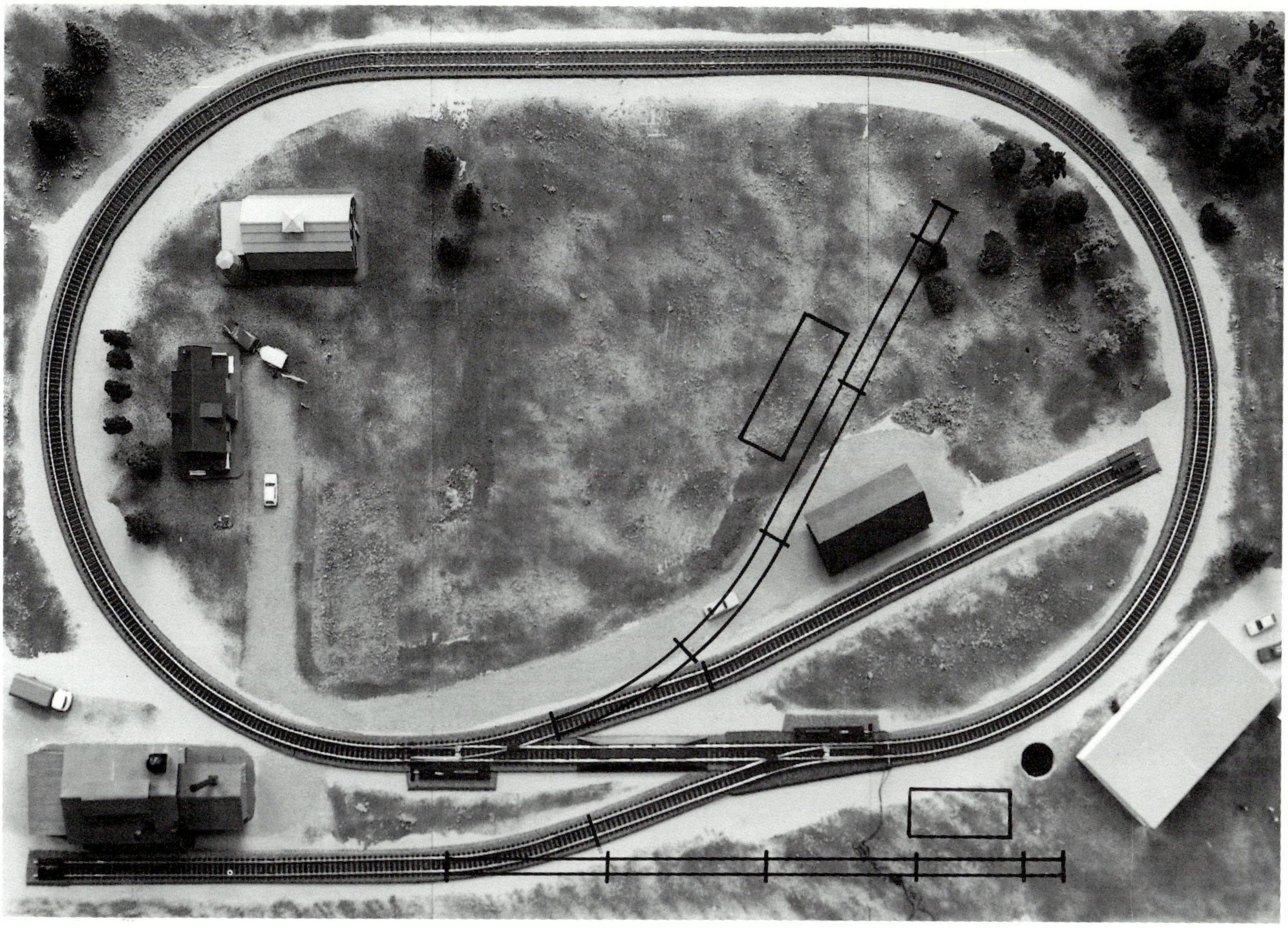

Here's one simple way to expand the Cornbelt Central.

aircraft
1 Model Power no. 465 pickle factory
Train Board
Lumber needed:
4 8′-long 1 x 3s
3 2 x 4-foot ½″ plywood panels
or
1 4 x 6-foot ½″ plywood panel
48 1½″ drywall screws
or
½″ pint white glue
and
1 box 1½″ nails
1 quart light tan flat latex interior wall paint

EXPANDING THE CORNBELT CENTRAL
Track needed
2 no. 860 switches
4 no. 150 straights
2 no. 843 bumpers
1 no. 823 3″ straight
1 no. 152 curve
small industry (your choice)

If you don't have any HO track, the Atlas starter set will get you off to a good start and save you money at the same time.

a spur to deliver crop-dusting chemicals and aviation fuel to the airport.

If you do add on, though, we hope you won't go overboard. Small layouts with too much track can actually become less attractive and interesting because they start to look too confusing. You can't figure out which track takes you where. The old pros call such layouts "spaghetti bowls."

The chapters on track, roadbed, and scenery cover how we added those two ingredients to the layout. We kept it simple and you'll have no problems if you decide to follow our lead.

Realistic roadbed is easy to add to your layout.

Roadbed

Lots of beginners want to use cork roadbed, even on their first layouts, because it makes the railroad look more attractive and realistic. The track looks as if it were laid on a specially prepared base, just as on the real thing.

Most modelers use cork, but other roadbed products are available to look at before you decide. One possibility in all the scales is foam strips that come with molded-in depressions for the ties. Matching foam castings are available to fit popular brands of switches. Mossmer is one popular brand.

Before laying the cork roadbed on our HO layout we assembled the track and double-checked it. We made sure our end curve was 36″ across (twice the 18″ radius). We nailed the track in enough places to keep it from sliding and test ran it.

Another alternative is to use a brand of track that comes with the roadbed already cast in. Kato's Unitrack, available in both HO and N, is an excellent product for the modeler who wants fine appearance with no more effort than snapping the track together.

Laying Cork

Cork roadbed is available in all the scales and comes in 3-foot strips. It's hard to see sometimes, but the strip is slit almost all the way through at an angle down the middle. To use it you separate the two halves.

The photos here, taken as we built our HO layout, show the basic steps in laying the cork. The only tricky part is turnouts, but take your time, work carefully, and you'll get good results.

One last word of advice. Cork roadbed, unlike sectional track, is not a product that can be taken up and reused. Hold off on laying the cork until you've gotten the hang of putting down good trackwork and have decided exactly what track plan you're going to build for a permanent layout.

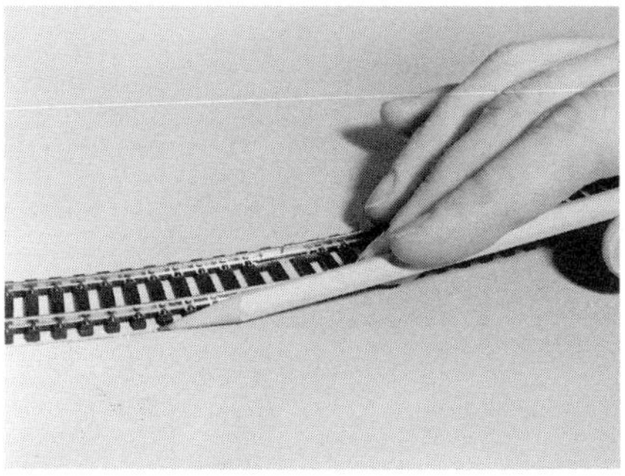

Outline the track with a pencil, holding it at a low angle so you can draw it smoothly across the ends of the ties.

A simple paper gauge marked the track center lines, which we then drew in.

Rather than just pull the cork strip halves apart, we separated them neatly with a hobby knife, held at an angle to match the slit in the cork.

We laid the cork with white glue (Elmer's is a familiar brand). You can also use track nails, one every three or four inches, but gluing goes faster. The glue grabs quickly, but you have about half a minute to position the cork. Ends on curves need to be tacked with a nail to hold them in place until the glue sets. Here we've already laid the inside of a curve, placing the vertical edge against the track center line. With the glue applied we're ready to lay the outside piece.

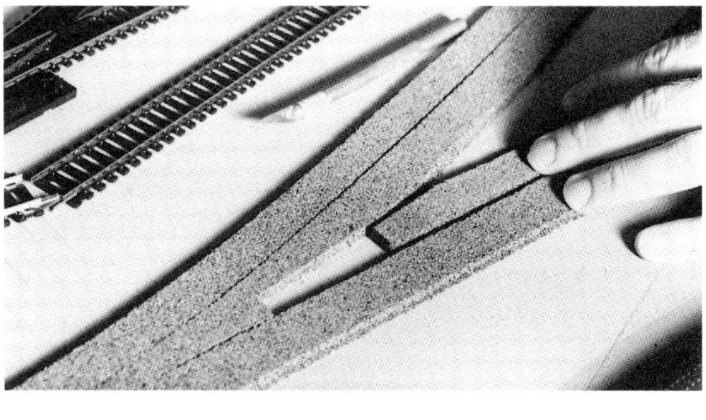

Laying roadbed for switches is tricky. Lay continuous strips alongside the outside first, then trim a piece to complete the curved leg. Fit the last piece by laying it over what you've done and cutting straight down through both pieces with a hobby knife, cutting the notch and the piece that fits into it at the same time.

For one switch we used this cork switch block. It cost only 57 cents and took the hard (also kind of fun) part out of the job altogether.

Smooth the corners on the finished roadbed with medium-grade sandpaper.

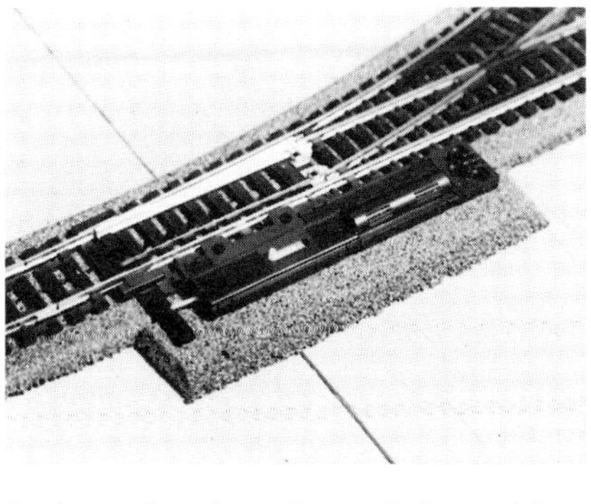

A piece of cork under switch machines dresses up their appearance.

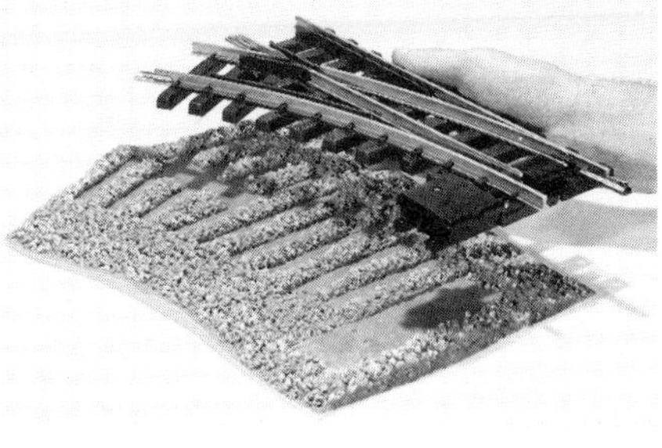

An LGB switch slips right into this foam casting by Mountains-in-Minutes. Similar instant roadbed materials are available in all the scales.

The scenery on our HO layout is simple, attractive, and beats the heck out of bare plywood. It was all done with the basic paint-and-sprinkle method described here.

Basic Scenery

Nothing transforms a train layout like scenery. All it takes is a little green grass and a tree or two and the old Plywood Central becomes a living, breathing railroad. Twenty years ago scenery used to strike terror in the hearts of modelers, but nowadays so many good techniques and products have been developed that fine-looking model railroad scenery is within the reach of everyone. If you can sprinkle salt and pepper on a steak, you can make nice scenery.

Ground Cover

By ground cover we mean just what you would probably guess we mean — dirt, grass, weeds — in short, stuff that covers the ground. For our purposes here, plywood cover might be a better name for it!

Before covering the ground you need to color it. We've found an excellent way to do that is with tan

To add ground cover we first painted an area with thinned tan latex paint. It's important to brush the paint on liberally and sprinkle on the ground foam before it has a chance to dry. We protected the track with masking tape.

Cast foam rocks are yet another scenery item you can buy. At left is one by Noch; center is one by Mountains-in-Minutes; right is one by Faller. The individual rocks up front are also by Faller. Some cast-plaster rocks by A. I. M. also sneaked into the photos. These can be stained and worked into the scenery.

Now that's a tunnel! This ready-to-run-through baby is for LGB-sized trains and made by Mountains-in-Minutes. Similar ready-made tunnels are offered in all the scales.

Scenery in a bag, that's ground foam. Stick it on the layout and it looks great.

paint. Let me emphasize the word "tan." The natural tendency for beginners is to pick a dark brown and they end up with scenery that's way too dark.

Inexpensive latex paint for interior wall painting works well. Make sure it's flat — you don't want glossy ground!

On every layout we built for this book we painted the train board as soon as we finished it, and three of them we painted with flat, tan latex. Painting the board before laying track or doing anything else saves you the problem later of trying to paint up neatly to the edges of the roadbed or the track.

Once the track was laid and we had a general idea of what our scenery would look like we used the tan paint, thinned this time, as an adhesive for our scenery materials. Thinning the paint (about 2 parts paint, 1 part water) allows it to soak into the materials and bond them better.

Ground Foam

The scenery material we employed throughout, and the one we recommend most heartily, is ground foam. Ground foam is literally latex foam rubber that has been ground up to various textures (coarse, medium, fine) and dyed various colors (most of them shades of green).

After painting an area with the thinned tan latex paint just sprinkle on the foam. Throwaway plastic or paper drinking cups make good dispensers. For best results add the foam lightly. The scenery will look more natural if the coverage is somewhat spotty and uneven and some of the paint shows through here and there.

To make sure the foam sticks brush the paint on very heavily so it will stay wet long enough to grab the foam. We found we could do about two square feet at a time.

Another secret of making nice scenery is using two or three shades and grades of green on an area so it doesn't look too uniform — what modelers have long called the golf-course look.

We used Woodland Scenics blended turf as a basic cover, added a Life-Like medium-grade bright green here and there, and finished with several light green shades of coarse foam. If you add the coarse stuff in clumps here and there it suggests patches of weeds or small bushes.

Once the paint had thoroughly dried we cleaned off the excess foam with a vacuum cleaner.

One beauty of this system is that if you find patches where the foam didn't stick or you just aren't happy with some area, you can easily do it over. Just paint right over the area with more thinned paint — you don't have to scrape off the previous application — and sprinkle on more ground foam.

If you have an area where the ground cover just doesn't want to stay put, you can fix it once and for all with dilute white glue. Thin the glue half-and-half with water and apply it carefully and fairly liberally with an eyedropper. It will seep into the area. Once it dries you won't see any glue, but the materials will be firmly bonded.

Trees, Rocks, and Such

The trees we used on our HO and N layouts came straight out of boxes bought at the hobby shop. We simply put blobs of white glue on the bases and stuck them on the layout.

Just about any scenery effect you can think of is offered as a commercial product by someone. You can even purchase a rock cliff — courtesy of Mountains-in-Minutes — that is painted and ready to build into your scenery. For that matter you can even buy bagged dirt, which is not as silly as it might sound. This dirt has been graded, baked to kill any spores that might start growing on your layout, and saves you the trouble of digging up your own yard.

And then there are the details: telephone poles, crossing gates, streetlights, cars and trucks, and most important of all — people. All these things are available in all the scales, and they add that vital ingredient to a model railroad — life.

Here's a basic 4 x 8-foot train board as recommended by KVal Hobbies in Buffalo, New York. The board is supported on a folding table too beat up to be useful for much else. Our Lionel Cannonball Express train set may look lonely out there in the middle, but peek at the photo on page 44 to see how we expanded from this humble beginning.

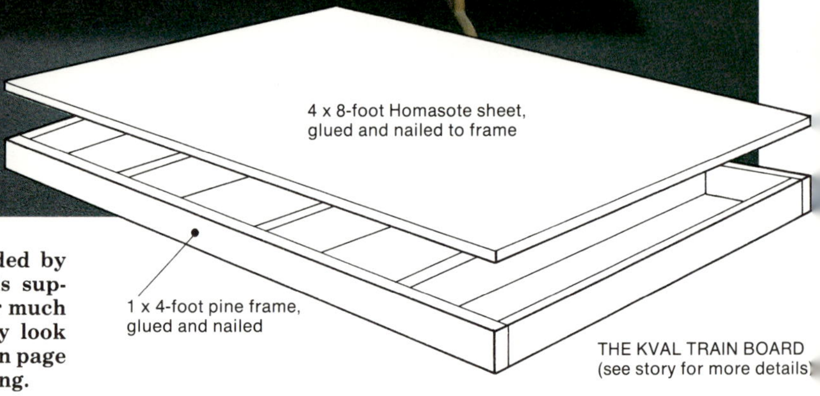

Train Boards

Running a train on your hands and knees can get mighty wearisome — even if you wear kneepads — so don't be surprised if the day comes quickly when you want to get the train up off the floor. Here we will show you some simple ways to accomplish just that.

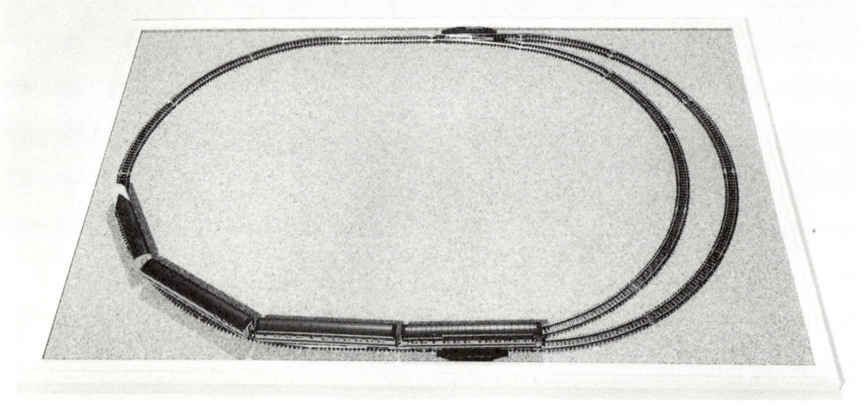

We purchased this 24″ x 36″ bulletin board on sale for only $8. It's just fine for a small, beginner's N scale railroad. Shop around and you probably will come across one big enough for HO.

The KVal Train Board

First comes a basic train board idea we got from Bob Schuh of KVal Hobbies in Buffalo, NY. KVal makes a bunch of these each year and sells them during the Christmas season. They're good for any size trains.

The top is a pressed-paper product called Homasote, made by the Homasote Corp. This is used as insulating board in building construction, so if you call the lumberyards in your area you should be able to locate it. If not, write the Homasote Corp., P. O. Box 7240, West Trenton, NJ 08628-0240, for information on where to find it in your area.

One problem with Homasote is that it expands and contracts a lot with changes in humidity. Painting the train board with several coats of green latex paint will help control this and also make the board look a lot better. Natural Homasote is a dismal gray — the color of the recycled newspaper from which it's made.

The beauty of Homasote is that you can push track-laying nails into it easily. Needle-nose pliers are ideal for doing so, but any pliers you might have around the house will do. Lots of beginners want to experiment with various track designs and this track board allows you to do so easily.

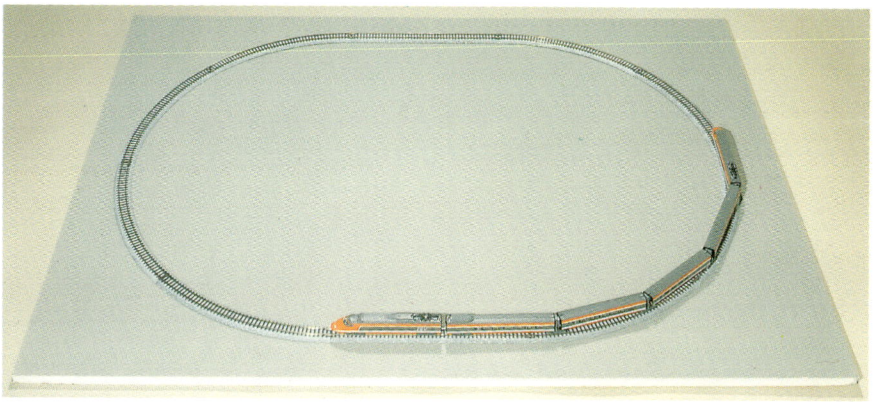

Foam-core board is available at art supply houses and comes in a variety of colors. For sufficient strength we recommend ½″ thickness. It's simply extruded Styrofoam with a sheet of paper laminated to each side. The paper provides just enough grip to hold track nails well. Used here with Kato's Unitrack system, foam-core board yields a simple, "high-tech-looking" railroad.

Other Train Board Ideas

Shoving a track nail into Homasote is about as easy as shoving a thumbtack into a bulletin board, which leads us to another suggestion — cork bulletin boards themselves. These come in a variety of sizes and are sold at office supply stores.

Less expensive ones are available at large retail outlets like K-Mart and Target. One of these would be particularly useful in N scale, and when not using it you might hang it on the wall — maybe even tack notes to it!

In the same category would be 2 x 4-foot ceiling tiles, used good side down. You can always find these on sale.

Lest we forget, thousands of trains have been set up on Ping-Pong tables. That's an old approach that still works great and makes the Ping-Pong even more exciting if you still play an occasional game!

Doors are another good possibility and surprisingly inexpensive. Take a look at our N scale project on page 28 for the lowdown on that.

Another good possibility for supporting a small train board is a card table. You can fold it up, hang the train board on the wall, and voila! the decks are cleared.

Larger folding tables, laundry tables or larger, also work well. Maybe you can find a bargain on one at a business furniture store.

Sawhorses are also great for supporting a train board and if you don't have any, lumberyards have inexpensive hardware and kits for making them.

And then another option is bookcases. Good-quality wood ones are expensive, but there are less-expensive options. Unpainted ones will save you money, and you can finish them for an attractive appearance.

Another good possibility is the paper-covered particle-board bookcases sold at large chain retail outlets. We bought several from Target, and you'll see how we used them with both our Lionel large-scale layout and our N scale railroad. One problem with these can be sagging shelves if you put a lot of weight (like lots of books) on them.

Plywood Train Boards

Eventually you may want to build a sturdier train board with a plywood top. We recommend ½″ plywood, 5-ply or heavier, for solid support. Too many modelers have tried lighter plywood, particularly three-ply material, and found themselves with a train board better suited to model roller-coastering. Look at our HO project on page 14 to see how we built our plywood train board.

We almost forgot — you could just add legs to your platform and make it into a table. Use straight 2 x 2 lumber and — very important — diagonal bracing. For strength we recommend using screws to put it all together.

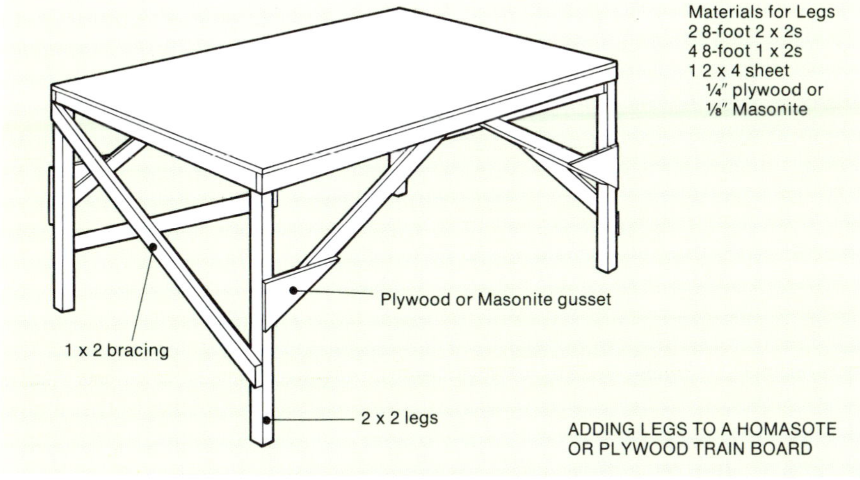

ADDING LEGS TO A HOMASOTE OR PLYWOOD TRAIN BOARD

Simple sawhorse kits are inexpensive. You can put them to their intended use while making a train board, then use them to support the finished project! Our kits yielded sawhorses 30″ high, a little too low for comfort. You might look for taller horses, or just purchase the hardware and cut your own 2 x 4 legs and crosspieces. A height of 40″ is comfortable for most people.

Our author couldn't resist the temptation to include a shot taken on his own home N scale layout. A. L. Schmidt photo.

Getting Started in N Scale

N scale trains were introduced in the late 1960s. Hobby dealers tell us about 20 percent of today's beginners are getting started with these small trains. At a proportion of 1:160 they are about half the size of HO trains (1:87), but appear much smaller because an individual model, say a locomotive, occupies only ⅛ as much space. You can easily hide an N scale switch engine in the palm of your hand.

Developed in Europe, N was called N because the rails were spaced nine millimeters (a little less than ⅜") apart. The word for nine in most European languages begins with N (*neuf* in French, *neun* in German), so they figured, "Heck, let's call it N!"

In those early days N was something of a novelty scale. We saw N layouts built in coffee tables, violin cases, and even on the brim of a hat. Soon, though, it became apparent that N's small size made it a natural for apartment dwellers and others who had room only for small layouts.

N Scale Products

N scale doesn't have the abundance of products available in HO, but still there's plenty to choose from. There are two useful catalogs for learning what's available. Your dealer might have these. If not, you can write for ordering information.

First is William K. Walthers' *The World of N & Z Scale.* Walthers is the United States' largest model train distributor, and its address is P. O. Box 18676, Milwaukee, WI 53218.

The second catalog is Con-Cor's *Trainalog*. Con-Cor's address is Box 328, Bensenville, IL 60106. It is a distributor, but also a major N scale manufacturer, particularly of N scale locomotives and cars.

The emphasis in N scale is on ready-to-run. Almost all locomotives and cars go straight from the box to the railroad. The modeler wanting to build locomotive or car kits will find few exist.

Unfortunately, N has one of the same problems HO does — low-quality train sets sold at Christmas. Notable exceptions are the fine train sets by Kadee, although these are likely to show up only in better hobby shops, not large retail outlets.

Although poor-quality locomotives have been at least as big a problem in N as in HO, lots of good engines have also been available. The locomotive situation has gotten even better in the past several years, particularly through the efforts of Kato, a Japanese firm that offers engines under its own brand name and also makes some for Atlas and Con-Cor. (Presently Kato makes all Atlas engines, but only some of Con-Cor's.)

Mini-Trix is another good line of engines that has been around for a long time. Presently these include some of the engines in the Model Power line and also some in Con-Cor's.

All N scale engines are imported, either from Europe or the Orient, and since some importing companies handle locomotives made by two or more different manufacturers, brand-name quality can be uneven. Manufacturer quality is more predictable. Your dealer should be able to help here.

Small, but mighty! That's N scale when in the hands of a master craftsman like Kent Lannert. This shot was taken on an Ntrak module that measures only 2 x 4 feet.

Your First Top-Quality Engine

A good locomotive for your first N scale engine would be Con-Cor's PA-1. It's heavy and has 12 powered wheels, all picking up current, so it will negotiate dirty track that would stop other engines. The PA-1 is an N scale classic that was introduced in 1967.

Speaking of track dirt, because N scale equipment is so small and light, keeping the track clean is even more important than it is for the other train sizes. For that reason we recommend against small engines, particularly industrial diesel switchers and tiny steam engines. It's just too frustrating to keep them running, particularly across switches with plastic frogs.

N scale modelers often pull their trains with two or more locomotives, even on small layouts, partially in response to the dirt problem, but also because it seems more natural and realistic in this small size. You seldom see diesel locomotives running singly in the real world.

Track and Cars

The line of N scale track and turnouts you're most likely to find in the shops is Atlas. These are good products, but sometimes you have to tune up some of the turnouts for better

Con-Cor's PA-1, made by Kato, is an N scale classic. We recommend it highly as a first locomotive.

This splendid N scale layout measures only 22″ x 46″. Bob Hood built it for display at father-in-law Erich Fuchs' hobby shop in Laconia, New Hampshire. Bob Hood photo.

Kato's GP50 is an excellent locomotive, representative of Kato's products.

performance. The procedures shown on page 4 should lead you to good running.

Almost all N scale cars are sold ready-to-run with what are called Rapido-style couplers. This coupler doesn't look realistic, but it does an excellent job of keeping trains together, and you can couple and uncouple the cars rather easily.

There are many excellent cars — Atlas, Roundhouse, Model Power, Life-Like, Bachmann, and Con-Cor all make nice ones. Almost all cars come with the coupler box and truck frames as a single plastic casting. (Cabooses tend to be an exception.)

If you have one car that's a chronic derailer, the most likely problem is wheels that aren't the correct distance apart on the axles; that is to say, they aren't in gauge. The National Model Railroad Association, which establishes standards for all the scales, offers an N scale gauge. Your hobby shop should have one, and for only a couple of bucks it's a sound investment for checking your wheels.

Among experienced N scale modelers a popular brand of cars is Kadee.

Some excited railfans have hopped from their car to take photos on Jim Whitehead's layout. Dave Frary photo.

These cars cost twice the price of other brands but have intricate detail. Unfortunately for the beginner, Kadee cars come equipped only with Kadee's couplers. Most advanced N scale modelers use these, and maybe someday you'll want to. Your dealer should have some he can show you.

Hobbies Within a Hobby

Kadee cars are popular with collectors, which leads us to note here that car and locomotive collecting is a popular sideline in N, more so than in HO. Maybe this has something to do with the small size — you can keep a large collection in a small space.

Another specialty interest in N scale is modular railroading. Modelers all over the country build small modules (usually 2 x 4 feet) that can be joined end to end like dominoes to make large display layouts. The first and foremost modular organization is Ntrak, a worldwide organization that got started in 1973. Ntrak layouts often feature trains more than a hundred cars long. For more information, write Ntrak, 2424 Alturas Road , Atascadero, CA 93422.

"Lots of railroad in a small space." That's the phrase you'll hear from N scale boosters all the time, and it's true. If you like your mountains tall and your trains long, that's what N scale does best.

Our N scale West Virginia Central is built on a hollow-core door. The controller rests on a simple plywood shelf screwed to the bottom.

The West Virginia Central

Bookcases work fine for supporting our N scale railroad.

Our N scale layout is built on an ordinary hollow-core interior door of the sort used in contemporary homes and apartments. These doors are readily available at lumberyards and home improvement stores and offer plenty of advantages for use as train boards.

Hollow-core doors are attractive, strong, and weigh practically nothing. For the person who has no tools and no penchant for carpentry they're ideal — construction time and effort have been reduced to zero.

The standard height for these doors is 6′8″, but they come in a range of widths, starting at 12″ and stepping up 2″ at a time to 36″, making them useful for N scale with the 9¾″ minimum radius we recommend, or for Lionel.

The widest door available is too narrow for HO or LGB, but you can dance around that problem by using

We ballasted and laid our track at the same time. Step one was painting the roadbed with a coat of tan latex paint.

Then we worked quickly but carefully to lay the track.

The ballast is fine gray from Woodland Scenics. Ballast is available in a variety of colors and grades from several manufacturers.

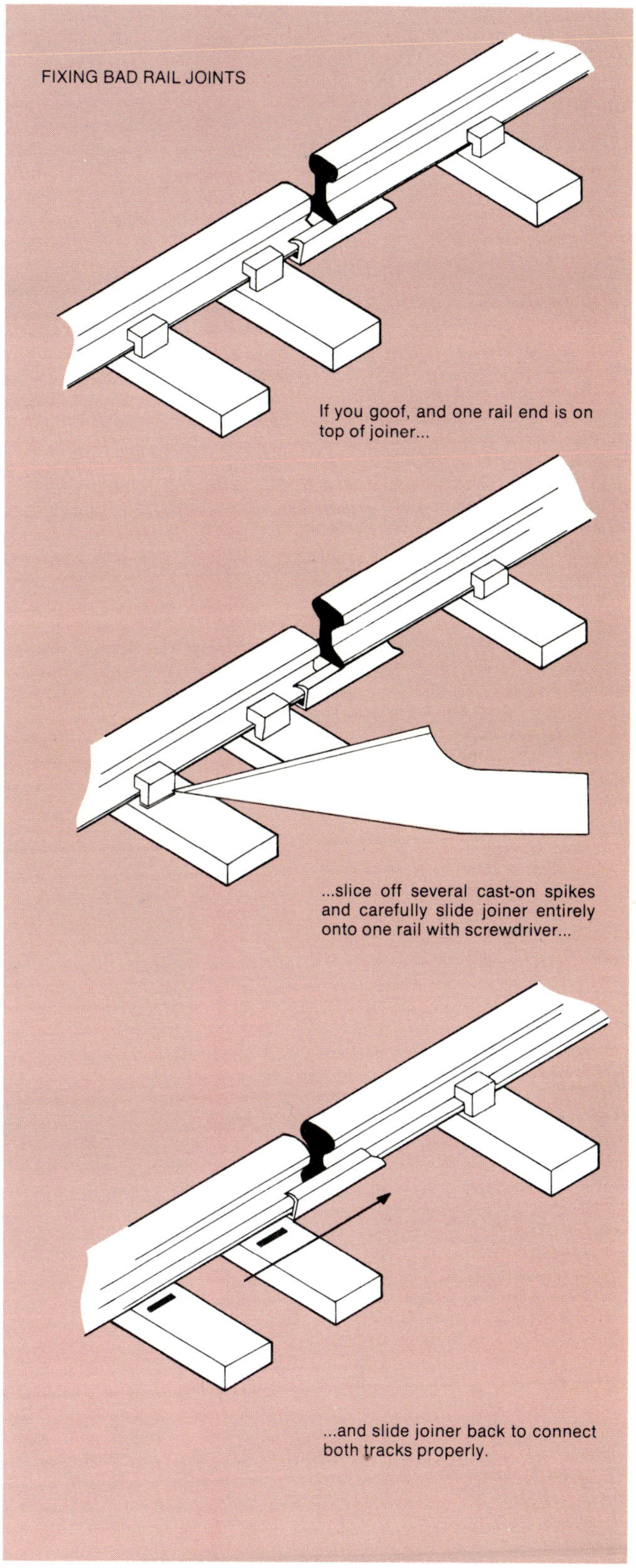

two together, as was done for our Two-Door LGB railroad shown on page 36.

Our N scale road was built on a 26″-wide door that cost us 15 dollars. If you're looking for a bargain, call some lumberyards and ask about damaged doors. Sometimes you can buy these for only a few dollars. Usually they've been banged up on only one side, so place that side down and you're in business.

Laying your track on a door is simple because of its construction. The surfaces are thin (1/8″) sheets of soft plywood, and because the core is usually hollow (except for some cardboard bracing) you can shove track nails in easily with a pair of needle-nose pliers.

Track

The overhead view shows the Atlas track pieces we used. This layout is more ambitious than our HO railroad (three switches plus a crossing).

Because the design is just a little more complex, we employed a variety of short fitter pieces to make it work out. A similar assortment of

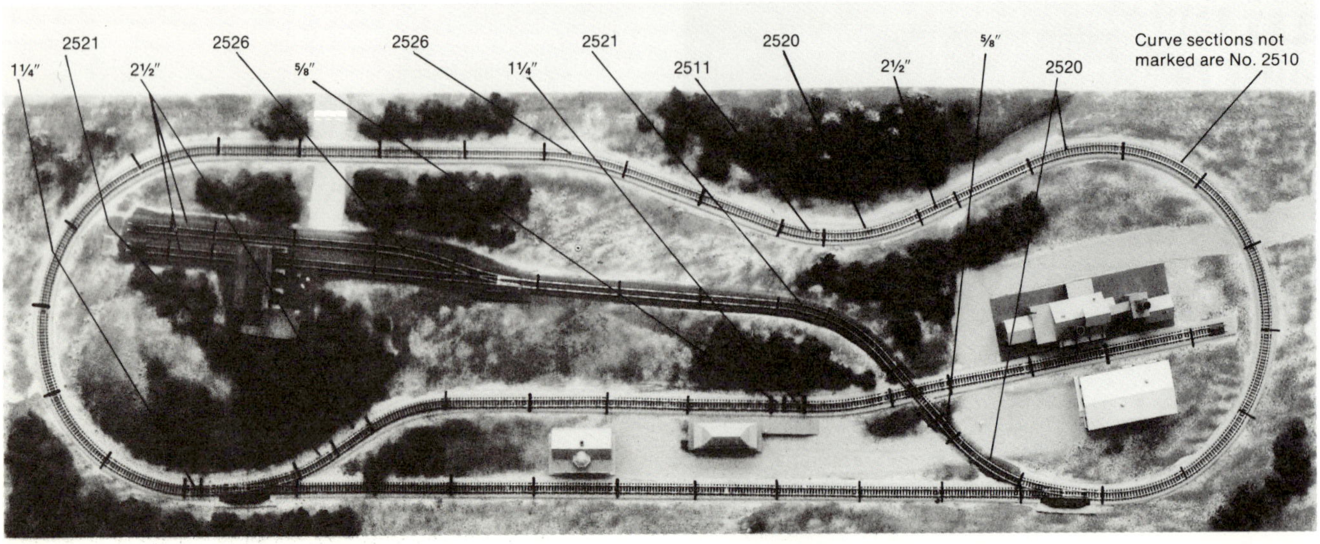

Here's the track you'll need for the West Virginia Central.

N SCALE WEST VIRGINIA CENTRAL

Track (all Atlas)

14 No. 2510, 9¾" radius curves
1 No. 2511, ½ 9¾" radius curves
3 No. 2520, 11" radius curves
3 No. 2526, 19" radius curves
2 No. 2521, ½" 11" radius curve
31 No. 2501, 5" straights
2 No. 2509, track assortments
2 No. 2536, track bumpers
1 No. 2568, 60° crossing
2 No. 25831, right-hand switches
1 No. 25821, left-hand switch
1 No. 2539, terminal joiners

Structures

1 Kibri No. 7982 gravel tipple
1 Micro Engineering No. 55001 Murphy Manufacturing
1 Con-Cor No. 002-00682 Jacobs Supply Co.
1 Con-Cor No. 002-649 station

It's easy to create a small N scale railroad that's business-like. Factories and warehouses in N take up no more space than homes or gas stations in HO.

For N scale you can make nice forests by cutting off the coarsest part of the plant and gluing the rest on the layout. We used a large (17.6 oz) bag of dark green by Vista Scenic Hobby Products. The lichen forest trick also works well with HO.

Our Baltimore & Ohio FA-1, by Roco, came in a set with four cars. Here it serves the coal mine that is the West Virginia Central's main source of business.

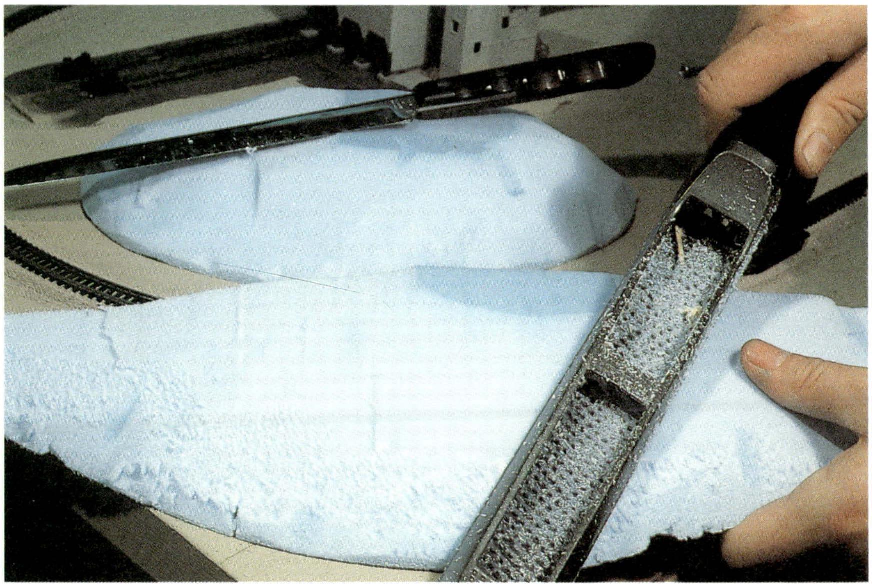

On the N scale layout we got adventuresome and added a couple of hills. These are carved from scraps of 2″-thick foam insulation. You can buy a sheet of this at the lumberyard, or keep your eyes open for useful scraps around construction projects. Kitchen knives are good for carving the foam. Here we're using a Surform tool to smooth it. A coarse file would also work. We used our tan latex paint to bond the hills to the layout.

short filters is also available for HO.

We added cork roadbed to this layout, using the techniques shown on page 18, then decided to go one step further and add rock ballast. (On a real railroad the ballast, usually crushed stone, holds the ties in place.)

Our method was simple. Doing about 18″ at a time, we painted the cork with full-strength tan latex paint then worked quickly to position the track pieces and nail them in a few places before sprinkling on ballast.

Lots of Lichen

One of the oldest and still champion model railroad scenery materials is lichen. This is a forest growth that has been processed so it won't dry out and is dyed green or some other color found in nature. (It's also dyed some screaming colors seldom seen out of doors on this planet, but we recommend you leave those on the dealer's shelf.)

G gauge's large size and old-time steam flavor remind us of earlier times in the worlds of both real and toy trains. Celebrated railroad modeler and photographer Malcolm Furlow captured the romance of G in this photo taken on his small indoor railroad. The engine is by LGB.

Getting Started in LGB and G Gauge

Finished buildings, ready to place on the layout, are rare in most scales, but you'll find them in G. Usually, as was the case with this gas station, completed buildings are limited editions.

Of the four train sizes we're discussing in this book G is the biggest, and when we say big, we mean BIG. These trains loom over the others like a truck over a bicycle.

This large size is also the newest, and there's still considerable confusion about what to call it. For the sake of simplicity we'll call it G gauge.

Big Train Background

LGB is a brand name used by the first and most widely known manufacturer of these large trains, Lehmann, located in Germany. The letters LGB stand for *Lehmann-Gross-Bahn*, which translates to Lehmann's Big Railroad.

Lehmann introduced LGB in 1968 and called the size G scale. These were to be high-quality, tough trains that would stand up to the punishment youngsters can dish out. They would be big and rugged enough to be used outdoors — for that matter left outdoors — so the G stood for Garden (*Garten* in German), as well as *Gross* (large). The track gauge was 1¾″.

Because of LGB's success lots of other manufacturers jumped into the G scale market. Not all of these use the same 1:22.5 scale ratio LGB does.

Russ Larson, editor of MODEL RAILROADER Magazine, has a G scale garden railway in his backyard. Here he's running Bachmann's radio-controlled Big Hauler. Photo by Barbara Larson.

Some use 1:24, some use 1:29, and some (like Lionel) don't consider scale important. Sometimes the manufacturer's goal is simply to design and build attractively proportioned trains the public will like and buy.

Despite these differences we can say that all trains that are LGB-compatible and intended to run on LGB track are G gauge. Don't expect to have the same kind of product interchangeability, though, that you find in HO or N. You may have to switch couplers or make other changes to run products of various manufacturers together. Delton is a source for conversion couplers.

Train Set Basics

You can forget our warnings about Christmas train sets when it comes to LGB's products. The LGB name is synonymous with quality, although that quality doesn't come cheap. The most basic LGB sets are $300 and up. These come with a basic 0-4-0 steam engine, two cars, a power pack, and a circle of track (12 curved sections).

When the time comes to go beyond the circle, several track expansion sets are available. These include one or two switches and some straight sections.

Although these are big trains (enormous, actually, when compared to the other trains in this book), you don't necessarily need a lot of room to run them. The basic curve radius is 24″, as compared to 18″ for HO, so figure roughly that the same layout that would require 4 x 8 feet in HO would require 6 x 12 feet in LGB.

LGB's catalog shows a wide range of locomotives and cars. Also there's a full line of sectional track similar in its geometry to what's available in HO and N. Structures and figures are also available.

Walthers' *The World of Large Scale Trains* is a catalog that includes LGB, but also all the other companies now in G gauge. Your hobby shop may have a copy, or you can write Walthers, P. O. Box 18676, Milwaukee, WI 53218, for price and information.

Beginners often assume that because these trains are so big they'll require massive power packs. Such is not the case, as these engines have efficient motors. Unless you expand a great deal the power pack that comes with an LGB set should meet your requirements. If you do decide to buy another pack, you should get one designed to handle LGB. LGB engines have 18-volt motors, but most power packs are designed for the maximum 12 volts used by locomotives in the other scales.

I wish we had a crystal ball. Right now G gauge is growing so quickly it is impossible to predict the place it will ultimately hold in the toy train hobby. The trains are big, colorful, and pack an abundance of charm. G gauge trains are tough enough for children to play with, yet detailed enough to interest adults. They are expensive, but have the quality and character that we think will make them popular with tomorrow's toy train collectors.

This deluxe Colorado & Southern 2-6-0 comes with sound, whistle, and smoke systems.

Kalamazoo has a complete line of locomotives and cars, including this 4-4-0 locomotive.

Our Long Horn Cactus Central is a 12-foot-long switching layout, using Lionel's Large Scale Gold Rush Special. The scenery is loose rock and live cactus.

The Long Horn Cactus Central

Large scale's main limitation is — surprise, surprise — its large size. This is neat stuff, but where do you put it if you don't have a garden or a large basement? After all, the basic track circle is a little too large even to fit on a standard, 4-foot-wide sheet of plywood.

Why not forget about the loop and run large scale along the walls as a shelf-style layout? We decided to give it a try, and the result was our Long Horn Cactus Central, a switching layout presentable enough to be set up in a family room. We also wanted to try live scenery — to bring the outdoors in with small cactuses from the local plant and garden center. This is garden railroading minus the bugs, sunburn, and sore knees!

The Basic Long Horn Module

The basic modules were made by mounting 2 x 4-foot ½″ plywood panels to frames made of 1 x 2s. The backdrops are foot-high ⅛″ Masonite panels painted with a deep blue flat latex paint (Fantasy Blue from Ace Hardware). Once the blue had a day to dry we painted on some mountains, using the same flat tan latex paint we used on the modules.

Our three modules are supported by an inexpensive ($40) bookcase from Target (an all-purpose discount store). We assembled them to one another temporarily with C clamps, but you'd want to bolt them together for a permanent installation.

Track

Our turnouts are by LGB. Some of the track sections are LGB and some are Lionel. Using them together is easy, following the directions and using the rail joiners that come with Lionel's boxes of four straight sections.

We didn't nail the track down. Gravity is more than sufficient to keep the pieces in place with this big stuff.

Live Scenery

Those big red rocks are exactly what they look like — big red rocks. They came from a garden center and are of the volcanic persuasion so they don't weigh much. We also bought a small bag of red volcanic rocks, a bag of pea gravel, and a few scoops of sand.

The cactuses also came from a garden center. I transplanted them from their small plastic pots, but you can just leave them in the pots and work the scenery up around them.

Just a dribble of water every week or two and some sunlight is all these hardy little plants need.

If you become really interested in indoor garden railroading a small book on the care and feeding of cactuses would seem to be in order. If you're running your Long Horn Cactus Central in the basement and sunlight is not available you may have to look into special plant-growing lights.

The Train Set

Our train is Lionel's Gold Rush Special train set with several additional cars. The cars are light and tended to derail when we backed them into the spurs. The solution, though, was easy. We added a little pea gravel load for extra weight.

The train set power pack just wouldn't run the engine slowly and smoothly enough for our purposes and gave us some scary moments. We didn't want to see that pretty engine plunge to the floor, so we hooked the layout up to our MRC 1400, which ran the engine beautifully.

Summing It Up

Switching cars on this layout is a lot of fun, especially because the knuckle couplers work well. We'd just push the trip pin up with a Popsicle stick to open them. Our layout is three modules (12-feet) long, but we tried basically the same thing in a two-module version and that was fun too.

With this approach you could make your large scale layout go just about anywhere in your home. If you already have a layout in one of the small scales you might enjoy this as a second layout and conversation piece.

When the time comes to move you'll have no worry about damaging the scenery. Just sweep it off into a couple of buckets and take it with you!

We carefully removed the cactuses from their plastic pots so as not to disturb the dirt around their roots. After setting them on the layout, we built up around the pot soil with sand, pea gravel, and rocks.

BASIC LONG HORN CACTUS CENTRAL MODULE

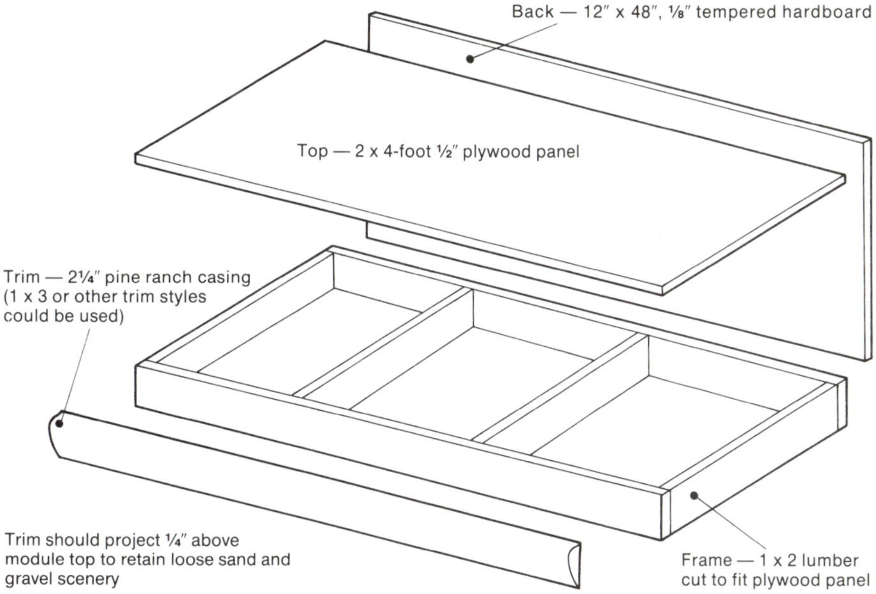

LONG HORN CACTUS CENTRAL TRACK PLAN

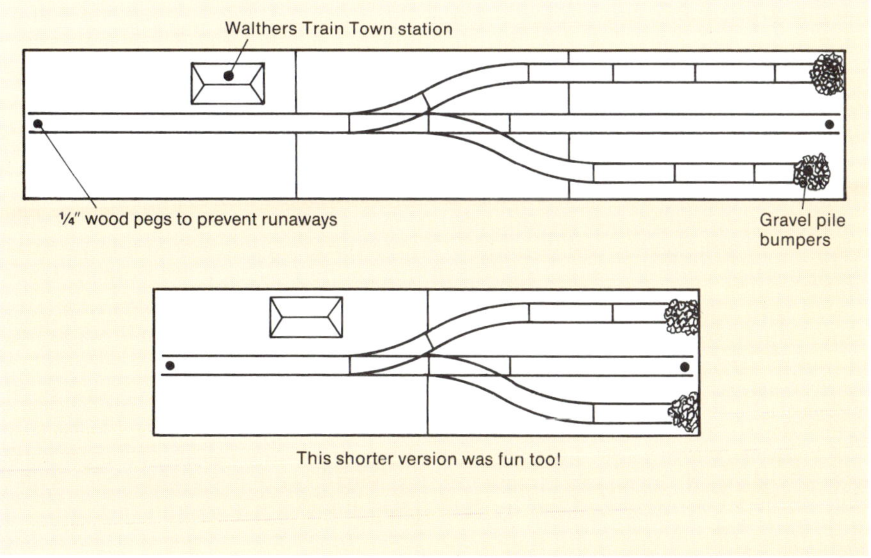

An LGB passenger train runs around our Two-Door RR. The layout is easy to build and folds in half for storage.

Build the Two-Door RR

Large-scale trains are great for small children, but since they are big they can take up a lot of room when set up in a permanent layout. We built the Two-Door RR as a portable, storable layout for G scale trains. It is made of two hollow-core doors joined with hinges and opens into a 5′0″ x 6′x 8″ setup.

The Two-Door RR can be used indoors or outdoors, on a table, on the floor or patio, or on a couple of sawhorses. There's even space to set up a Christmas tree in the middle. It quickly folds to just 4¾″ x 30″ x 6′8″ to be put away in a closet, garage, or utility room. Everything you'll need to build the Two-Door RR is listed in the bill of materials.

We started out by setting the two doors edge to edge on a flat surface and screwing on the hinges. The offset hinges swing the doors further apart when you fold them together, to make room for the two thicknesses of track that end up sandwiched in between.

At first we thought we'd need some sort of spacers or bumpers to protect the tracks, but that wasn't necessary. The rails simply come together and the track is more than sturdy enough for this kind of treatment — the LGB catalog shows an elephant walking on it.

Be sure to put the two end hinges right at the edges of the doors to clear the track and the trains. Put the two center hinges where their screws will go into the solid wood where locks would be installed. The handles make the layout easier to move, and one refinement that we didn't add would be a hook or latch to hold the doors closed for carrying.

When we had this "carpentry" done we painted the doors a bright, grassy green on top and a warm terra-cotta around the edges. If you want to set up a layout on a nice table or floor you might want to add something on the underside for protection. We looked at rubber toilet seat bumpers as candidates for this job, but strips of felt or old carpeting would be good, too.

Next we put the track loosely in place as shown in the track plan, with the expandable sections fully extended, and drew lines ½″ wider than the ties all around to mark out our "roadbed." Then we took the track up again and painted the roadbed gray, and also laid out and painted the road (terra-cotta). Use masking tape to get neat, sharp color separations.

That's all we did for "scenery." We wanted the Two-Door RR to be neat and presentable, but we didn't want a realistic "scale model" effect. This is supposed to be a place for kids to play with their toys and use their imaginations.

After the paint dried we replaced the track and screwed it down with small wood screws. The track is equipped with holes in the ties for this, and you can press a scriber or sharp ice pick through them into the wood to start the screws. You can place the terminal connectors — for wires to the power pack — on any track section, but they should be in place before you fasten that section down.

Don't screw down the expandable sections or the last straight section on the spur track. You'll be able to retract the expandable sections and lift them out when you want to put the layout away, and the straight section from the end of the spur can

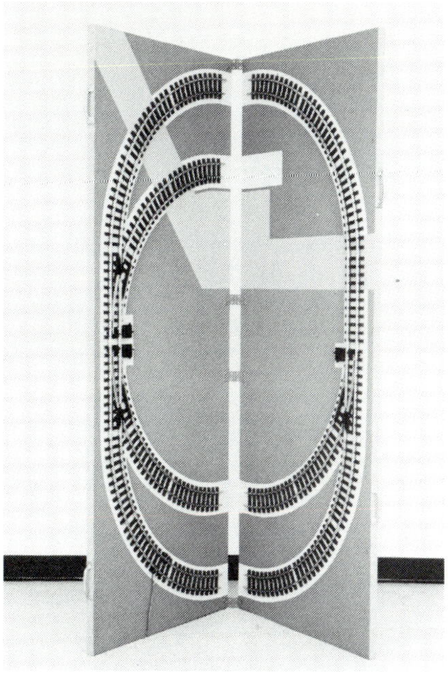

With the expandable sections and the end of the spur removed, the Two-Door RR folds right up.

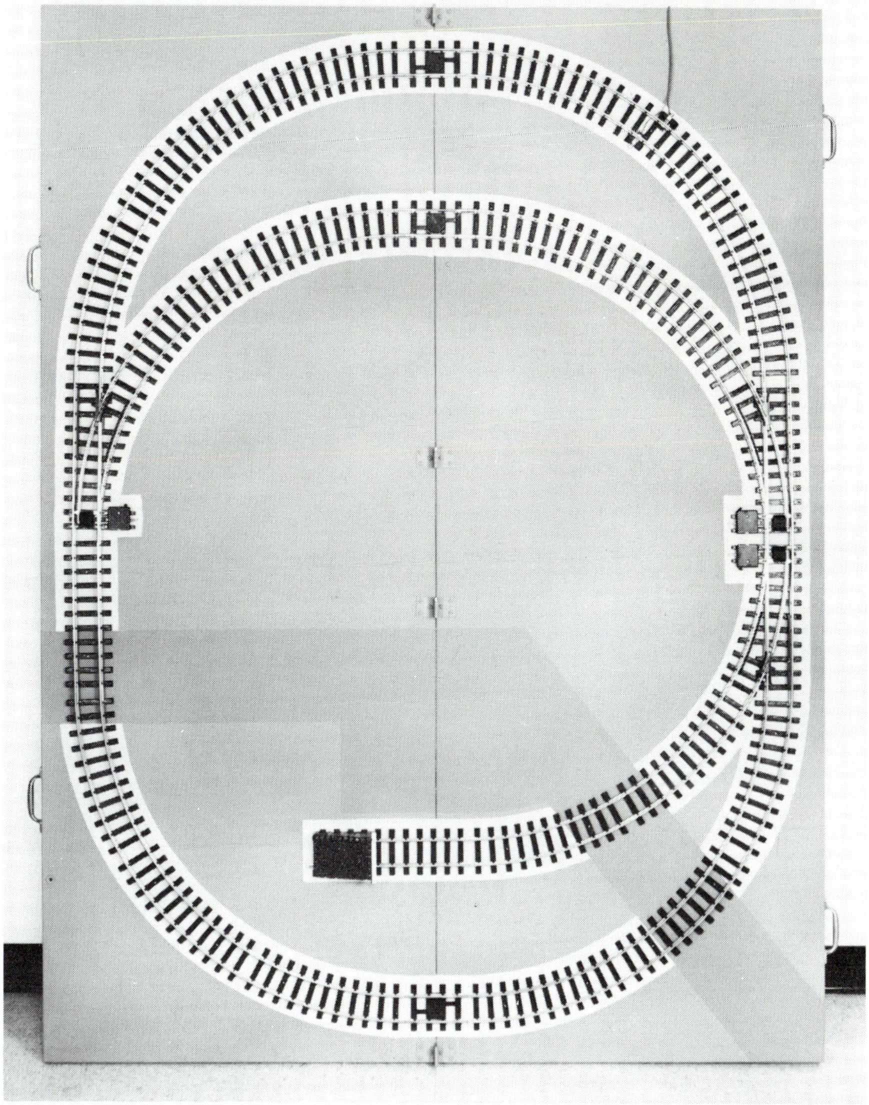

be pulled off with the buffer stop (bumper) in place.

It took us just three or four hours to build the Two-Door RR, and it's a simple enough project to let your children help with. You can use the same layout for Kalamazoo and Playmobile trains as well, and you can use the two-door construction with a different track plan for a Faller or Lionel train set.

BILL OF MATERIALS

LGB track and train set

3 1009 expandable track sections
2 1100 curved track sections
20301 U. S. Passenger Starter Set
20901 Buffers track expansion set
20902 Station track expansion set

Hardware and paint

2 30″ x 6′-8″ hollow-core doors
4 ¾″ offset hinges (with screws)
4 3″ bronze door/drawer handles (with screws)
50 No. 1 x ½″ round-head brass wood screws (for track)
1 qt. green flat indoor latex paint
1 qt. gray flat indoor latex paint
1 qt. terra-cotta flat indoor latex paint

Optional items (as in photos)

Ceji-Revell Digger Dan 6 x 6 truck with crane trailer and container
LGB 4021 open goods wagon
LGB 4033 closed goods wagon
Scankit 2510 railway station plastic assembly kit(Con-Cor International, P.O. Box 328, Bensenville,IL 60106)

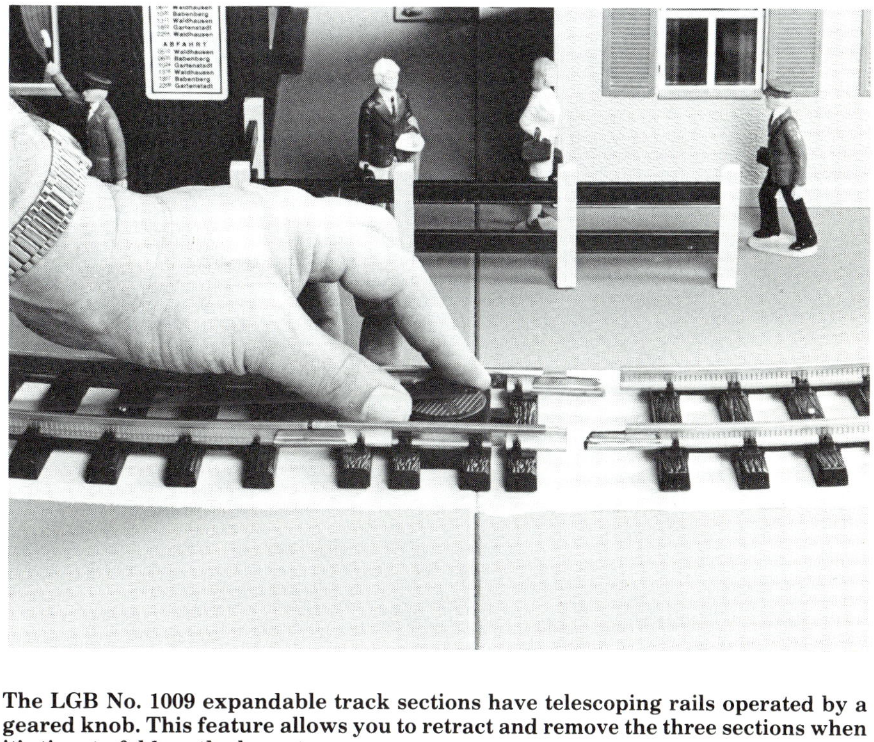

The LGB No. 1009 expandable track sections have telescoping rails operated by a geared knob. This feature allows you to retract and remove the three sections when it's time to fold up the layout.

Electricity

The heart of a model railroad is the power pack. Not all train sets come with one, but you must have one to run the train. From the power pack you need two wires running to the track, one to each rail. Make sure you connect them to the correct power pack terminals, which might be labeled *trains* or *variable DC*. If you accidentally connect them to the *AC* terminals, sometimes marked *Accessories*, your locomotive will probably emit a puff of smoke, curl its toes, and die.

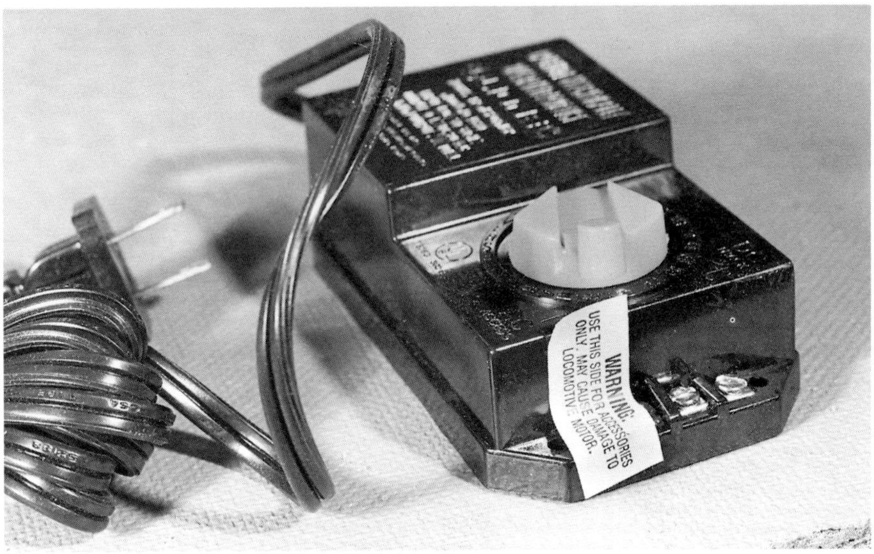

Lionel placed a warning label on this train set power pack to make sure the purchaser didn't connect track wires to wrong terminals. Both AC and DC locomotives are available in the Lionel line, so you three-railers should be doubly careful.

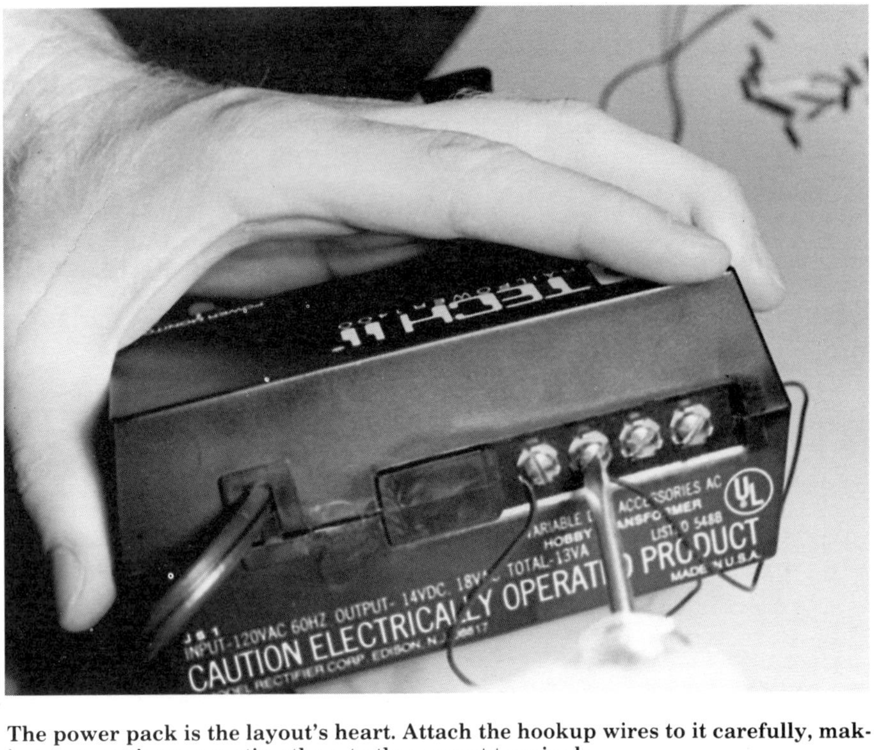

The power pack is the layout's heart. Attach the hookup wires to it carefully, making sure you're connecting them to the correct terminals.

If the power pack terminals use screws, make sure the bare wire ends are neatly curved and tucked under them. Be particularly careful with stranded wire and twist the ends. Be sure there are no individual strands waving around that might touch the other wire or terminal post and cause a short circuit (more about that later).

Connecting your hook-up wires to the rails is usually easy because the train set includes a track clip of some sort, a terminal track, or at least a pair of rail joiners with the wires soldered to them. If perchance you're starting without a loop of train set track you can buy terminal joiners or terminal track sections at your hobby shop.

When the Train Won't Go

If the train won't go, first check to make sure the power pack is plugged in. If you still can't get any action, plug a lamp or a radio into the wall outlet to see if it's working. If it's not you may have blown a fuse or tripped a circuit breaker in your house wiring and will have to attend to that.

If the wall outlet is live, wait five minutes and plug the power pack in again. Beyond that there's little you can do. Assuming the track and engine wheels are clean, something is the matter with your power pack or your engine.

Whatever you do, don't even think about taking the cover off your power pack and trying to fix it. The power coming out of the pack is harmless — you probably can lay your finger across your tracks and not even feel it — but the power from the wall circuit to the pack can kill you.

Train Set Power Packs

"Do you think I need a new power pack?" That's one of the questions hobby dealers often hear from beginners who've gotten started with train sets. Often the answer is yes. That doesn't necessarily mean that train set packs are bad. Usually they're fine for what they're designed to do — run the engine and cars that came with the set on the small loop of track included. It's just that they may lack the power to do much more.

As our layouts grow we tend also to run longer trains. Because the engine has to work harder it needs more power, and here again the set pack may not be able to deliver.

Sometimes it's difficult to run the train smoothly with a train set pack because the speed control knob or handle works stiffly and has a short range of travel. Also some set packs don't have a direction switch. Instead, there's a center-off position with reverse to one side, forward to the other. You try to slow to a smooth stop and just when you think you've succeeded, go ripping off in the other direction!

Replacement Power Packs

A good replacement pack should have enough power for future growth. We suggest at least 1 amp for any small, say 4 x 8-foot, layout. The speed control should work smoothly. Many dealers suggest the MRC Railpower 1400 as a good replacement pack.

By the way, don't throw your old power pack away. You can use it to power switch machines, streetlights, or other electrical accessories.

Beginners frequently ask about the "speedometer numbers" printed on power pack faces. They don't mean a thing. Moving the controller up to 50 doesn't mean the train is going 50 mph or anything else. The numbers just make the pack look a little more businesslike and they do give you some frame of reference. With experience you'll know at what settings certain of your engines start moving.

When buying a new pack be sure to tell your dealer what scale trains you're running. Some power packs cannot be used with N scale because even when the speed controller is turned all the way down they're still putting out enough power to keep those little guys going. Also, if you're using the large sizes you generally need a more powerful pack. Discuss it with your dealer.

How Your Train Works

For your train to run the power must go out from the pack along one wire, pass through the engine, and come back to the pack along the second wire. Lionel's three-rail system is a little different. Think of the current as going out to either of the outside rails and coming back from the middle one.

It's important to understand that this electrical path, called a circuit, must be complete. If the circuit is broken anywhere no current flows and the motor in the locomotive won't work. Electricians call this an open circuit. The most likely cause of an open circuit on a train layout is dirty track and wheels. Other possibilities are broken or burnt-through wires in the engine or power pack, or rail joiners that aren't making good contact.

Short Circuits

The other electrical difficulty you can have — and one that's more difficult to explain — is the short circuit. Perhaps you've already created one or two by accidentally laying a screwdriver or some other metal object across the tracks. Usually you'll see some sparking, then nothing as your power pack shuts down to protect itself.

To explain this in a most nontechnical way, electricity is lazy stuff and seeks the path of least resistance. If it can complete a circuit without having to do any work — making a motor turn or a lightbulb light — that's what it'll do.

The problem with a short circuit is that without a load (motor, lightbulb, or other device that makes something useful from electricity) there's nothing to limit the amount of current flowing. All the energy the pack can produce is set loose, creating heat. The energy will keep flowing until the circuit is finally broken — we hope by a fuse or a circuit breaker. Otherwise we can burn out the locomotive's motor, our power pack, or even start a fire.

Short circuits on model railroads can be created by anything that conducts electricity and bridges the cir-

'LECTRIC LINGO

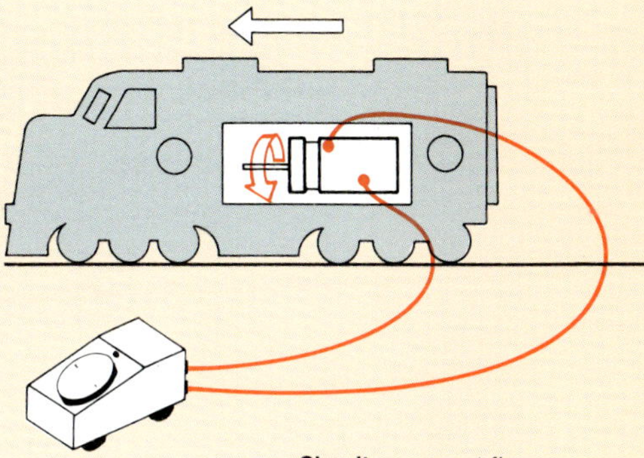

Circuit — current flows and train runs

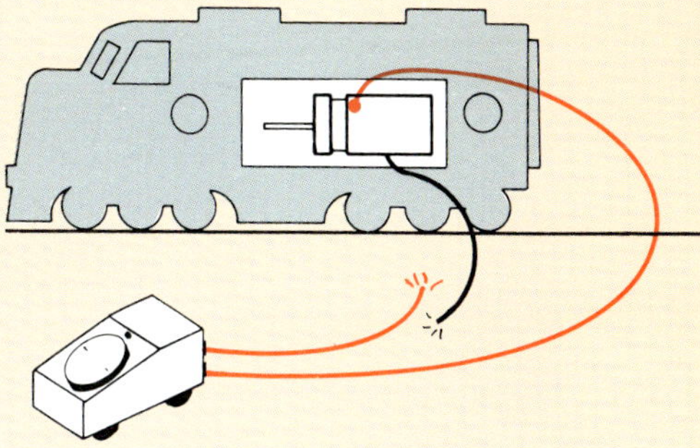

Open circuit — no current flow

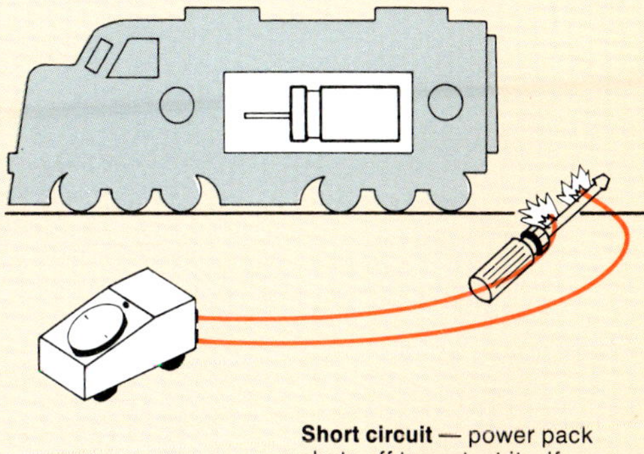

Short circuit — power pack shuts off to protect itself

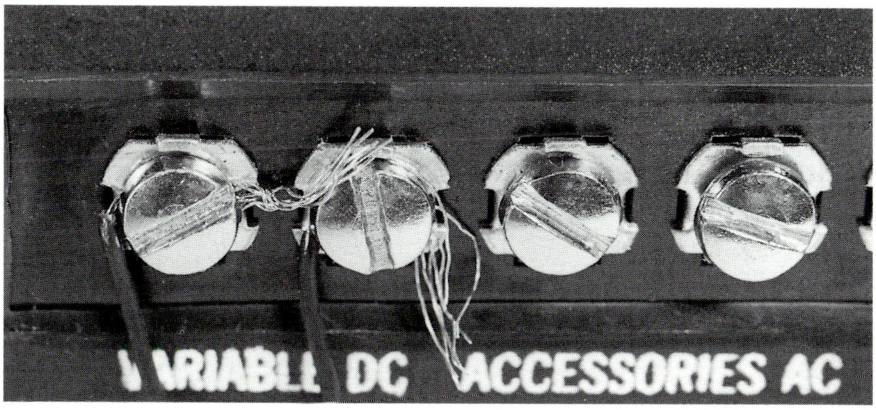

This is the most common electrical problem we see. Loose wire strands are bridging the terminals, causing a short circuit.

cuit on either side of the load. Until you've found the cause of the short circuit and removed it, the train isn't going to go anywhere. Once the cause is removed, the circuit breaker inside the power pack will reset and you'll be back in business. Until then the pack will just keep shutting down every time you turn it on.

The Return Loop Problem

This brief discussion of short circuits leads us to some understanding of a trap that awaits the unwary. Once you've made a loop of track, it's the most natural thing in the world to want to build a diagonal cutoff across it. That way you could run the train around the loop in one direction for a while, then cross the loop on the cutoff and reverse your direction. Unfortunately with two-rail track you can't do it without getting into more advanced wiring. (You Lionel guys have got it made on this one.)

Look at the reverse loop diagram and you can see you've built a direct short circuit into the layout. The rail we have labeled plus (+) runs headfirst into the rail we've labeled minus (−). Oops! One rail can't be on both sides of the circuit at the same time.

This diagram shows another fatal reverse loop. The basic rule in working out any track plan is that the train can never double back on itself if you want to run the layout with just one set of feeder wires. Trace your finger along the route. If you find a stretch of track where the train would be going the opposite direction from what it was going before, you've found a fatal reverse loop.

Keep in mind that we're not saying reverse loops are impossible. They're just impossible if you want to run your layout with one simple set of hookup wires. Advanced electrical topics like return loops and running two or more trains at the same time are covered in our more advanced books.

THE REVERSE LOOP PROBLEM

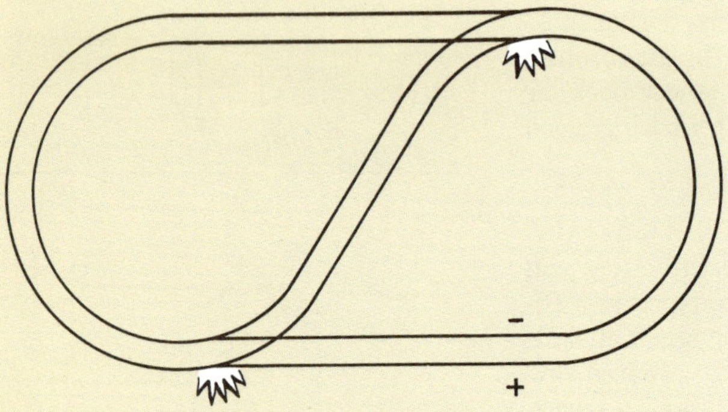

You can't do this in HO, N, or G without special wiring.

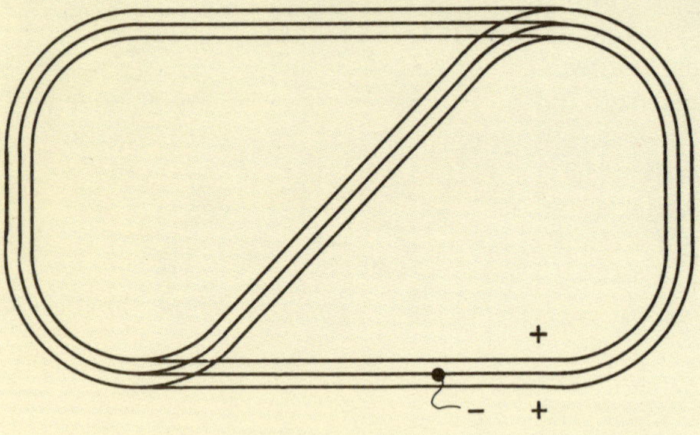

With Lionel, you can. (We did on page 42, and the train ran fine.)

Here's a typical short circuit. The steel axle on the pilot wheels is touching both the outside and center rails.

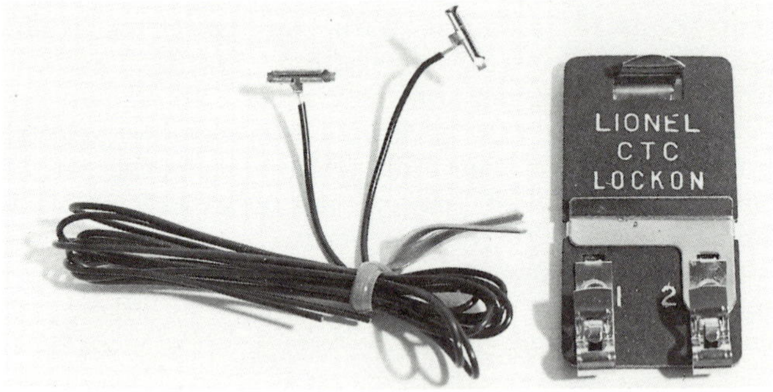

It's easy to connect the hookup wires to the track. Left is a pair of terminal rail joiners. These are available in both HO and N. Right is Lionel's track clip, which is even easier to use.

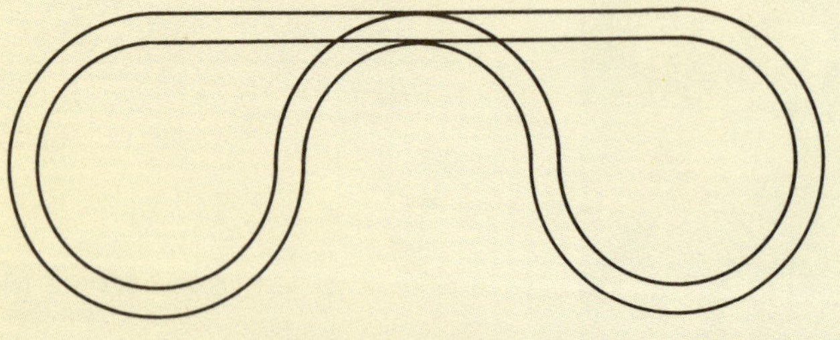

You can't do this in HO, N, or G without special wiring.

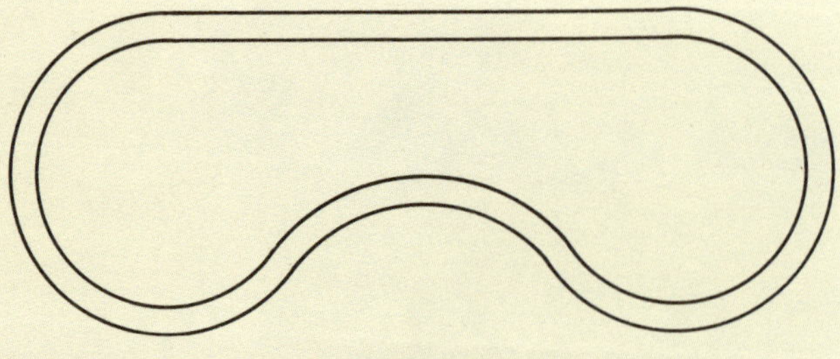

You can do this.

Plastic Structures

These gorgeous O scale structures by Lionel are representative of the fine offerings today in all the electric train scales.

Usually it isn't long before beginners want to add buildings to the layout. And the buildings most of us start with are simple, inexpensive, injection-molded plastic kits. Lots of these are available for all the train sizes we're covering in this book.

In N scale Bachmann offers attractive buildings that don't even have to be assembled. You just take them out of the box and plunk them on the railroad. No ready-to-plunk buildings are available in HO; however, International Hobby Corp. has some excellent snap-together buildings. Pola makes some beautiful LGB-sized buildings (ready-built or kit) that can be left out in the weather the year round.

Lots of you have built plastic cars and airplanes so are old pros, but here are a few tips for assembling plastic kits in any scale:

- Take your time. Because plastic kits are easy, we tend to think we'll just shake the box a few times and everything will fall into place.
- Don't twist and tear the parts from the sprues in the manner of a lion having lunch. Use a little tenderness. Fingernail clippers are excellent for clipping parts away neatly so as to avoid any damage. Hobby knives are also good.
- Make sure the pieces fit properly. Sometimes flash or little nubbins get in the way and need to be carefully trimmed away with a hobby knife.
- Use a liquid cement for plastics, rather than the gooey stuff that comes in tubes. One popular brand is Testors. The nice thing about these liquid cements is they don't add anything physical to the model. They are in fact solvents and work by softening the mating surfaces and bonding them together.
- Use enough solvent, but not too much, applied with a clean paint brush. (By using brushes of different sizes you can vary the amount of solvent being applied.) Obviously, this is a bit like being told to add some sugar to the cookie dough (like how much?), but it's hard to be more specific. You want the surfaces to bond well, so your structure doesn't fall apart later, but you also want a neat job with no distortion. (Incidentally, if you do get extra solvent on a surface, the best thing to do is just leave it alone. Usually when it dries it doesn't look too bad.)
- Don't throw the plastic molding trees away until you are completely finished with the project. That chimney or other final detail you are looking for is probably still on there! You just did not see it the first time around.

Check surfaces to be cemented for burrs or flash that would prevent a tight joint. Scrape the offending material away with a hobby knife.

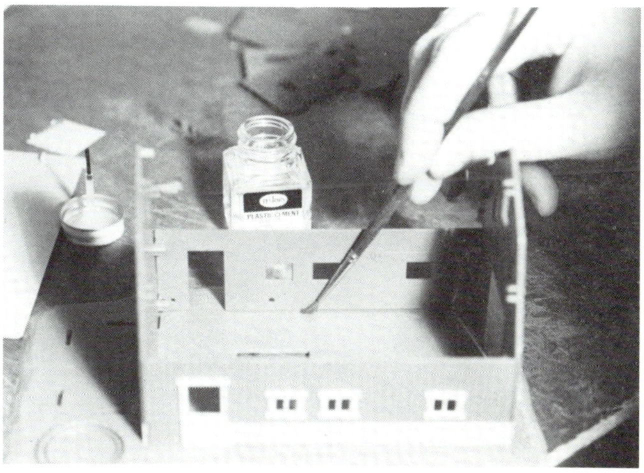

Liquid cement for plastics does a neat job; it can be applied with a small brush.

This scene was shot on a Lionel layout that travels the country in a 46-foot highway trailer. Andy Sperandeo photo.

Getting Started in Lionel O27

FIRST LIONEL CENTRAL
Track
8 027 straights
17 027 curves
2 027 right-hand switches
1 027 left-hand switch

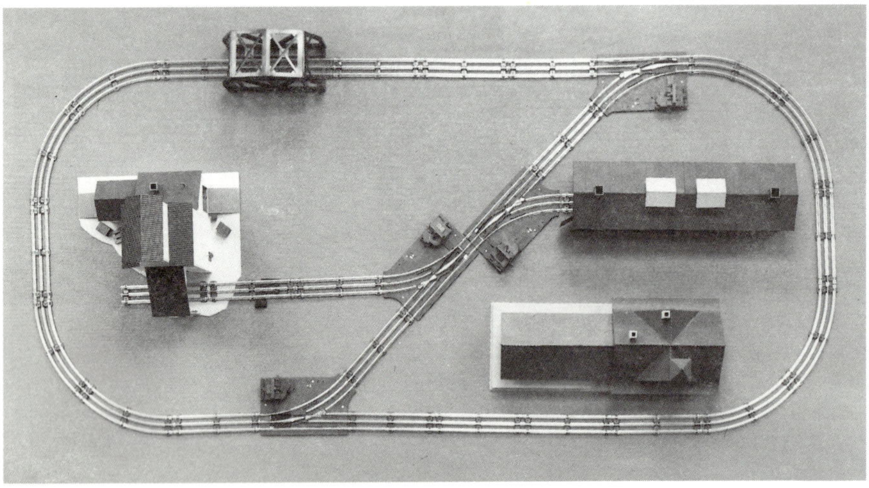

Our O27 layout has grown considerably from its humble beginnings. We've added four switches, more track, and three absolutely gorgeous Lionel buildings.

In the thirties, forties, and fifties when boys and girls dreamed of a model train running under the Christmas tree, the name they imagined on the side of the engine was usually *Lionel.* They mooned over Lionel's colorful catalogs the way gardeners study seed catalogs in the winter.

Lionel trains were big, went fast, made lots of noise, and were built to outlast the kids who ran them. The track with the third rail down the middle didn't seem to bother most children, and perhaps even helped give Lionel its special identity.

During the sixties and seventies Lionel trains came upon hard times and the products often weren't up to the old standard. The line changed ownership more than once.

In the eighties, under new ownership, Lionel returned to the quality of the fifties — in fact many of the locomotives and cars are made from the same tooling. New O gauge products are being introduced and at the same time Lionel is entering the large train (G gauge) market. Here, though, we'll just take a look at the O27.

O Gauge and O Scale

O track measures 1¼″ between the railheads and is a toy train gauge that goes back nearly to the turn of the century. Although nowadays we call it O (pronounced oh), originally it was given the number designation zero because it was so small compared to the number 3, 2, and 1 sizes then manufactured!

Lionel O gauge trains are by no means the only ones that run on O gauge track. Also available are O scale (¼″ = 1′) model trains that are altogether different and run on scale two-rail track. It is possible to adapt Lionel trains to O scale use, and vice versa, but Lionel trains are designed for the toy train market and may or may not be faithful scale replicas. Generally they are shorter than scale models and not so highly detailed.

In toys ruggedness, color, and play value are more important considerations. Details that would be delicate enough to break off are either fattened up or left off.

Big Trains in Small Spaces

So much for the O part in O27. Now we'll look at the "27" part. Almost certainly the track you get started with in Lionel will be its O27 line. It takes eight O27 curves to make a 27″-diameter circle. The minimum radius, then, is 13½″ and the amazing consequence of this is that you can build the equivalent O27 layout in less space than is required for HO!

As we pointed out in the electrical section, Lionel's three-rail trains work differently from the two-rail trains found in the other sizes. Think of it this way: Either outside rail can feed electricity into the motor. After going through the motor the electrical path back to the transformer is completed via the middle rail. (Turn a Lionel engine over and you will see rollers on the bottom that contact the center rail.)

As we pointed out, the reversing loops that are taboo with two-rail trains are no problem with Lionel, and we built one into our layout just to prove the point. With Lionel any track configuration you put together can be powered with just two wires running to the track.

Incidentally, you may hear the term "tinplate" used in reference to Lionel and other classic toy trains. This refers to the 1930s and before, when these toys usually were made from thin steel coated with tin (the same material used to make tin cans). The name has stuck and is even used in referring to modern toy trains, which are almost always cast in plastic. (One interesting note is that today Lionel offers stamped tinplate reproductions of some of its own trains from the twenties and thirties.)

Lionel

Lionel track can be difficult to put together, particularly for youngsters, as the connecting pins fit quite tightly in the rail ends. One tip when having difficulty is to wear gloves so you can get a better grip, also so you won't have so much difficulty with the tie ends and other fairly sharp edges. Run a pin into each rail end individually before trying to slide all three pins in at once.

Avoid the temptation to wiggle the pins back and forth, forcing the openings in the ends of the rail larger. Eventually the distortion could lead to derailments (although it takes one heck of an obstruction to derail a Lionel train). The more likely problem would be loss of good electrical contact.

The most recent Lionel catalog will keep you up to date on what's available. If your hobby dealer doesn't have a Lionel catalog, write to Lionel Trains, Box 746, Mt. Clemens, MI 48045. There's a full line of sectional track and also switches in both manual and electrical remote control versions.

Also there are remote control uncouplers. Automatic coupling and uncoupling is an activity that works well in Lionel (better than in the smaller sizes, actually), and curiously, Lionel's couplers are the most realistic of those that come standard with any train size discussed in this book.

Also useful is a book from Lionel called *The Lionel Train Book*, written by Robert Schleicher.

The Company with a Middle Name

In 1901 Joshua Lionel Cowen was an ambitious young man looking to start a successful business. A tinkerer, he was developing several promising possibilities: dry cell batteries, flashlights, and a small battery-powered fan.

His experience with these devices led him to try yet another product — a display electric train to run on a circle of track in a store window. The idea was to place merchandise on the train and display it in an eye-catching way. The electric car was a simple box on wheels powered by an electric motor from the fan project and some of Cowen's own batteries. It was painted bright red and lettered "Electric Express."

Many customers looked beyond the merchandise on the train to the train itself and wanted to buy that. Cowen realized he had stumbled onto something good, formed the company to which he gave his middle name, and started making toy trains. America's famous toy train company was born.

Although the terms O27 and Lionel are virtually synonymous, another manufacturer of O27-size locomotives, cars, track, and other accessories is MDK (K-Line).

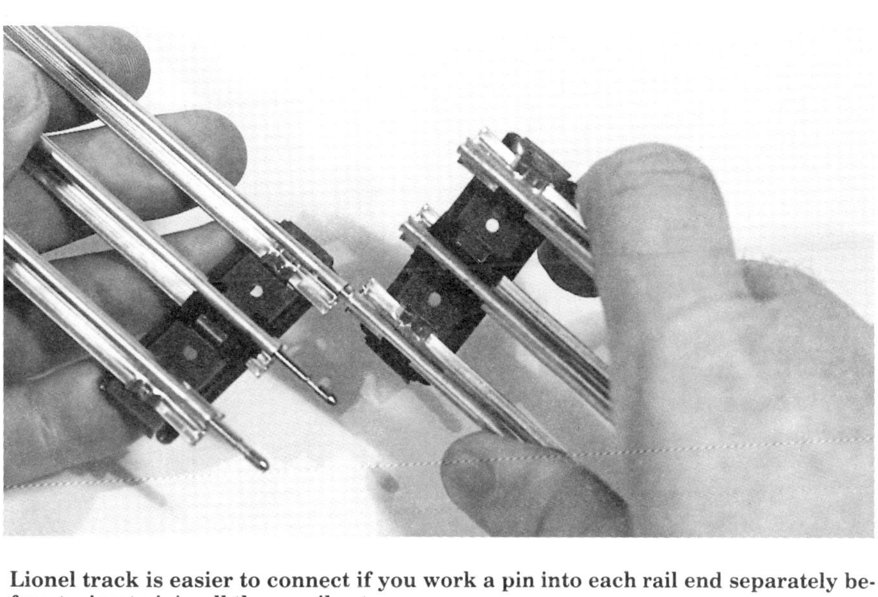

Lionel track is easier to connect if you work a pin into each rail end separately before trying to join all three rails at once.

PRAIRIE CITY
FEED & GRAIN
LIONEL

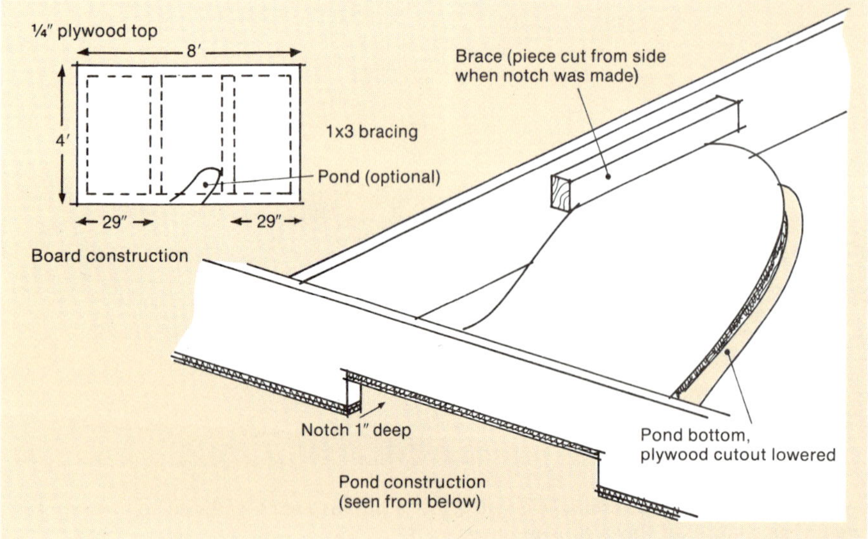
¼″ plywood top
8′
4′
1x3 bracing
Pond (optional)
← 29″ →
← 29″ →
Board construction
Brace (piece cut from side
when notch was made)
Notch 1″ deep
Pond bottom,
plywood cutout lowered
Pond construction
(seen from below)

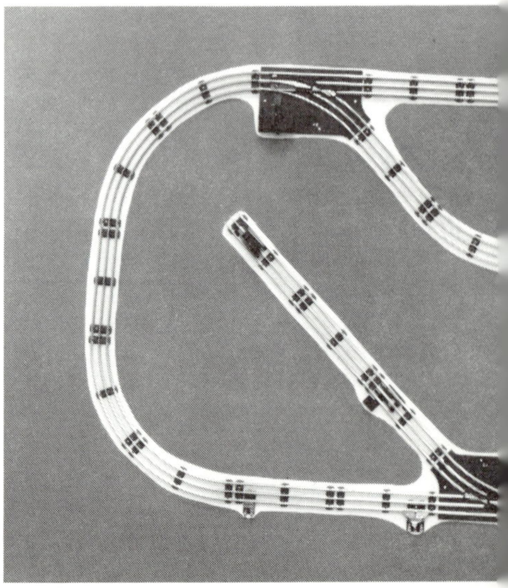

Building Your First O27 Layout

The ingredients for getting started in toy and model trains are simple. Take an O27 Lionel train set, add a few switches and some extra track, and build yourself a layout on a 4 x 8-foot sheet of plywood. Lionel trains are big, but with the tight (13½" radius) O27 curves, it's amazing how elaborate a layout you can build on a standard plywood sheet. Use this track plan if you like, make up your own, or pick one from the Lionel instruction manual that came with your train set.

We wanted a layout that could be leaned against the wall or stored out of the way when not in use. There are no legs — you can run the railroad on the floor or set it on a bed or a table. Since our layout was to be portable we made it as lightweight as possible by using ¼" plywood. This is flimsy stuff as it comes from the lumberyard but plenty strong enough once nailed and glued to a simple frame of pine 1 x 3s.

You could represent a pond or river by just painting it blue on a flat top, but we decided to get a little fancy and make ours lower than the track. The pond construction drawing shows how we did it. If you decide to build a pond too, lay your track out on the board and mark where the water area should go. Cut along the shoreline with a power saber saw. (If you decide to do more cutting in the board than we have, you should make your top of ½" plywood for extra strength.) We painted our pond blue, then lined the edges with broken bits of ceiling tile to represent rocks.

We painted our layout with two coats of yellow semigloss latex paint, let it dry, then mounted the track with small screws. The grassy areas we painted with two coats of semigloss bright green latex, leaving about an inch of yellow alongside the track to represent roadbed.

One plastic Lionel building was used on the layout, but we made three other buildings from cardboard.

Adding cars, trucks, and other details was lots of fun. We found quite a few highway vehicles at the toy and variety stores that are just about the right size. The two lines we like a lot are Buddy L and Tootsie Toy. Both are inexpensive, about $2 for an automobile, and their stamped metal construction and bright colors give them a traditional look that is right at home with Lionel trains. We would not dream of gluing them down — they are fun to play with too.

It would be easy to add another spur or two to the layout, and eventually you could extend it by buying another sheet of plywood and running tracks over to it. There's no hurry, though. For now it's lots of fun to watch that big train pound around the layout, every now and then stopping to switch a car at one of our industries.

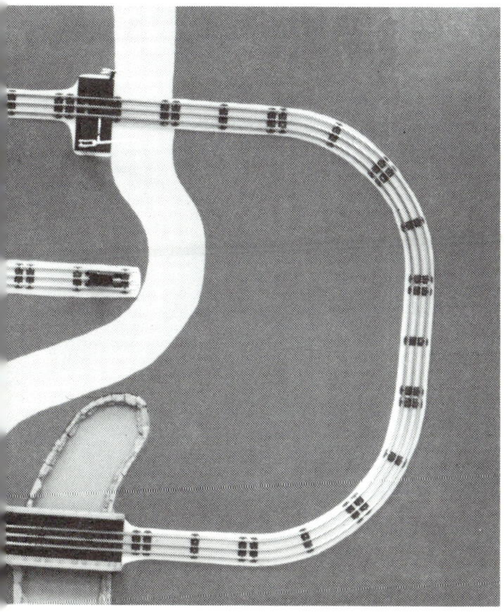

WHAT WE USED

Lionel No. 6-1602 Nickel Plate Special train set

Extra track

1 Lionel No. 6-5019 curved track (8 are included in set above)

14 Lionel No. 6-5019 straight tracks (4 are included in set above)

2 Lionel No. 605022 right-hand switches

Accessories

2 Lionel No. 6-12715 illuminated bumpers

1 Lionel No. 6-2214 girder bridge

1 Lionel No. 6-2784 freight platform

Lumber

1 4 x 8 foot sheet ¼" plywood

4 8-foot-long 1 x 3s

1 pint Elmer's Glue-All

1 pound 1½" finishing nails

Seems like one of the first things folks like to add to a train layout is a mountain with a tunnel. We got the urge, too, and built a simple one for our 4 x 8-foot O27 layout, introduced on page 44. (You can also buy ready-made tunnels at toy and hobby stores.)

Our tunnel is made of 2″-thick foam insulation material, also called beadboard. It's available at lumberyards and building centers. A 2 x 8-foot sheet costs about $5 and will make a mountain the size of ours with plenty of material left over.

As the photos show, we cut out layers of foam to make the mountain, like making a wedding cake. To mark where the track needed to go through the bottom layer we painted the two outside rails heavily with tempera paint then positioned our bottom layer and pressed it down before the paint had a chance to dry. An impression of the rails was stamped onto the foam and gave us an indication of where to cut.

Cutting the foam with a cake knife is not too difficult if you work slowly so as to cut through the foam beads, rather than tearing them out. We cemented the foam pieces together using Contech PL200 construction adhesive in a caulking gun.

To complete the mountain we did a little carving around the tunnel entrances to suggest rocks, then sprayed the entrances with Pactra Light Earth paint from a spray can. The rest of the mountain we painted with the same green latex paint we'd used on the O27 layout.

Add a Tunnel to Your Layout

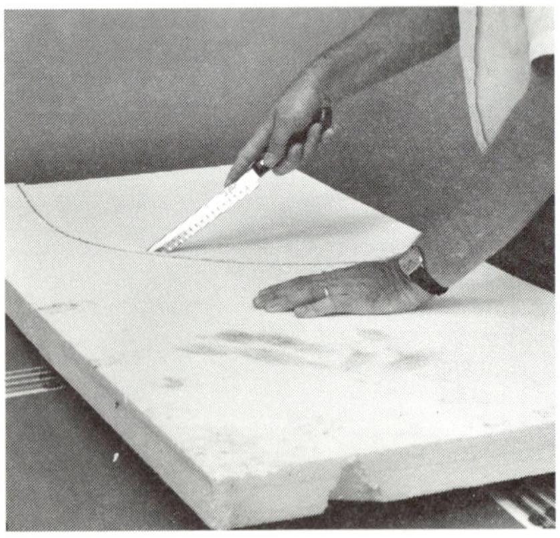

We cut the beadboard with a cake knife.

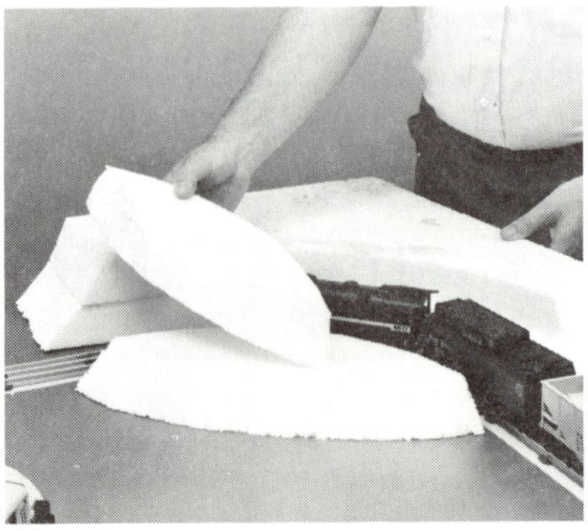

Foam pieces were piled up like layers in a wedding cake.

PL200 (by Contech) costs about $1.50 per tube, won't attack foam.

For some readers that first electric train will open the way to a lifetime of hobby pleasure. The Milwaukee, Racine & Troy, built by the staff of MODEL RAILROADER Magazine, took more than 12 years to complete. But like every other layout, from the magnificent module built by Kent Lannert on page 25 to our own Cornbelt Central, it had to begin with nothing but an empty space and a dream.

Moving on Down the Line

In this book we've tried to answer basic questions, the ones hobby dealers say they hear asked time and time again.

This book will take some of you as far as you're interested in going in the electric train hobby. For others we've barely scratched the surface. If you want to know more we suggest you invest in another book or two. The hobby shop where you bought this book should also have these:

All Aboard: The Practical Guide to HO Model Railroading: This book covers basic subjects beyond the scope of this book, among them, wiring for running two trains on the layout at the same time, wiring reversing loops, ballasting track, and building more complicated layouts with grades. Although the book covers only HO, much of the basic information is also valid for N and G. We recommend this book as the best follow-up to the one you're now reading.

Beginner's Guide to N Scale Model Railroading: As its title suggests, this is a specialized book for those working in N scale.

If you want to build some great-looking mountains, rivers, and other natural wonders right off, then we recommend *How to Build Realistic Model Railroad Scenery* by Dave Frary. This book covers all the latest techniques. If you follow Dave's careful directions you cannot go wrong. All the materials Dave uses are water-soluble, so they are safe and compatible.

If you're beginning to think about that big dream model railroad then John Armstrong's *Track Planning for Realistic Operation* will prove fascinating. Basically John explains full-sized railroading and how the real thing can be translated into model terms.

To keep up with new developments we recommend a monthly magazine: MODEL RAILROADER, published by Kalmbach Publishing Co. Issues run close to 200 pages and cover all the train sizes. Articles range from rudimentary information for beginners to sophisticated construction articles on everything from scratch-building cars to building your own control system.

Each issue features at least one visit to a beautiful model railroad, with big color photos and ideas you can employ on your own railroad. Another important feature is announcements and reviews of new products.

We hope the future holds many years of fun with electric trains for you.

Learn a Little Railroad Lingo!

Ballast. On real railroads the ballast is the crushed rock spread beneath and around the ties of track to help hold the track in place and provide for drainage.
Benchwork. The table or other supporting framework employed to raise a model railroad layout off the floor.
Branch line. A secondary line of a railroad, one that runs somewhere other than the main destination.
Cab. Another name for a model train speed and direction controller.
Caboose. The last car in a freight train, where crew members live and work while the train is in motion.
Couplers. The devices that hold cars and locomotives together.
Crossing. An arrangement where two tracks cross one another at the same level without connecting.
Crossover. An arrangement of two track switches connecting parallel tracks that allows a train to change from one track to the other. A double crossover allows changing tracks from either direction.
Derailment. When a train jumps the track.
Feeder. A wire that carries electricity from a power supply to the track.
Flange. The raised portion of a railroad wheel that runs inside the rails to keep the wheel on the track.
Gap. A break in the rails, usually to electrically isolate one part of a model railroad from another.
Gauge. The width of railroad track, defined as the distance between the insides of the rails. Standard gauge in North America is 4′ 8½″, but other railroads around the world employ both narrower and wider gauges.
Gondola. An open-top car for carrying things like coal or scrap metal. Gondolas have solid bottoms, and must be unloaded by cranes or by rotating them upside down to discharge their contents.
Grade. An ascending or descending stretch of track.
Hopper. A car for transporting bulk commodities, such as coal or grain, that are loaded into the car from the top and discharged from doors in the bottom.
Main line. The primary route of a railroad between two points. The term is usually used to distinguish an important route from a lesser one (usually called a branch line).
Power pack. A controller that reduces house current to a safe voltage, changes it to direct current (DC), and regulates the output to the track to control train speed. You'll need a power pack for trains that are operated by direct current.
Prototype. A term railroad modelers use to describe the real thing — full-size trains.
Rail joiner. The device that aligns and connects mating track sections. Rail joiners furnish mechanical as well as electrical continuity between track sections. Damaged joiners are often responsible for derailments or lack of electrical power to a track section.
Reefer. A refrigerated car used to prevent perishable foods from spoiling. The first refrigerator cars had to be loaded with big blocks of ice to keep the contents cool; nowadays they have their own refrigeration units.
Return loop. A switch and track section arrangement that changes the direction of travel of a train running through it.
Roadbed. The support beneath the track. On model railroads this is often strips of cork nailed down to raise the track off its baseboard.
Rolling stock. The engines and cars of a real or model railroad.
Roundhouse. A round or pie-shaped building used to house locomotives. The shape was a result of arranging the building to correspond with the tracks radiating from a turntable, which was used to turn steam locomotives end-for-end.
Scale. The proportion of a toy or model train to the real thing after which it is modeled, usually shown as a fraction or ratio, with the proportional size of the model on the bottom. The common toy train and model railroad scales are as follows:

- G scale: 1:22.5
- No. 1 scale: 1:32
- O scale: 1:48
- S scale: 1:64
- HO scale: 1:87
- N scale: 1:160
- Z scale: 1:220

Siding. A track that branches off from a main line and then returns to it. Such an arrangement permits one train to pass another or allows an engine to run around one or more cars of its train.
Spur. A track that branches off from the main line and ends at a bumper or other stub ending.
Switch. An arrangement of movable rails that allows a train to be diverted off to the left or right of the main route.
Switcher. A small locomotive used primarily for sorting cars in a yard. A lot of model locomotives are switchers because they can go around sharp curves and are good for small layouts.
Switch machine. A mechanical or electrical device that changes the track route through a switch or turnout.
Tender. A car that trails behind a steam locomotive to carry fuel (coal and oil) and water supplies.
Ties. The heavy cross members to which the steel rails are attached to make railroad track. On real railroads these can be wood or concrete.
Transformer. A controller that reduces (or transforms) house current to a safe current for operating model trains, and that allows regulating their speed. Transformers are used for trains that are powered by alternating current (AC).
Trestle. An elevated support that holds up track from below with posts and cross bracing, called bents.
Trucks. The swiveling assembly under a model car or locomotive that holds the wheels.
Turnout. Another name for a track switch.
Turntable. A track mounted on a rotating bridge, used for turning locomotives end-for-end.